SILENT ILLUMINATION

Silent Illumination

A Chan Buddhist Path to Natural Awakening

Guo Gu

SHAMBHALA

Shambhala Publications, Inc.
4720 Walnut Street
Boulder, Colorado 80301
www.shambhala.com

Cover art: Blue Collectors (Stocksy)
Cover design: Daniel Urban-Brown
Interior design: Gopa & Ted2, Inc.

9 8 7 6 5 4 3 2 1

First Edition
Printed in the United States of America

♾This edition is printed on acid-free paper that meets the American National Standards Institute z39.48 Standard.
♻This book is printed on 30% postconsumer recycled paper.
For more information please visit www.shambhala.com.
Shambhala Publications is distributed worldwide by Penguin Random House, Inc., and its subsidiaries.

LIBRARY OF CONGRESS CATALOGING-IN-PUBLICATION DATA
Names: Yu, Jimmy, 1968– author. | Zhengjue, 1091–1157. Works. Selections. English.
Title: Silent illumination: a chan Buddhist path to natural awakening / Guo Gu.
Description: First edition. | Boulder, Colorado: Shambhala, 2021. | Includes bibliographical references and index.
Identifiers: LCCN 2020013805 | ISBN 9781611808728 (trade paperback)
Subjects: LCSH: Enlightenment (Zen Buddhism)—Early works to 1800. | Meditation—Zen Buddhism—Early works to 1800. | Zhengjue, 1091–1157.
Classification: LCC BQ9288.Y8 2021 | DDC 294.3/4435—dc23
LC record available at https://lccn.loc.gov/2020013805

Contents

PREFACE

THE EVER-EXPANDING number of books in English on Buddhism and mindfulness are shaping the way we talk about meditation. This phenomenon is a real testament to the ways in which people everywhere are increasingly recognizing the benefits of meditation. However, the majority of these publications reveal more about Western ideas about spiritual well-being than the core teachings of buddhadharma: genuine awakening and liberation from suffering.

Chan Buddhism clarifies what awakening is and shows how to transform everyday experiences into the path. Distilled from centuries of development, Chan is the culmination and fulfillment of the Buddha's original message. However, the essence of Chan is largely absent from existing publications on Buddhism in the West, and this is especially true of the teaching on silent illumination.

The term *chan* comes from the Sanskrit word for meditation—*dhyana*—but in our tradition, the same word has evolved to include the realization of awakening to our true nature: our buddha-nature. The teaching on silent illumination, or *mozhao*, as it is called in Chinese, is both a metaphor for this awakened nature and the principle behind meditation practice.

The central tenet of Chan is that we are already free. It is only through our self-referential grasping and rejecting that our natural awakened nature is concealed. To practice Chan is to engage with the complexity of daily life in order to expose the places where we are stuck and, by working through and letting go of them, reveal this true nature.

Some years ago, my teacher, the late master Sheng Yen (1931–2009), published an introductory book devoted to silent illumination, *The Method of No Method,* based on his commentary to Master Hongzhi Zhengjue's (1091–1157) teachings. I translated several excerpts from Hongzhi's discourse records, helped to edit the book, and prepared it for publication. The present volume is an in-depth teaching on silent illumination and contains my own revised translations and commentary on Hongzhi's text.

The aims of this book are, first, to establish silent illumination squarely within the Mahayana Buddhist traditions. Second, to offer detailed instructions for establishing a foundation for realizing silent illumination. Third, to offer quality translations of Hongzhi's poetic writings on silent illumination. My comments on Hongzhi's writing aim to clarify any confusion practitioners might have about silent illumination, its breadth, depth, and perfection in seated meditation and in daily life.

The book is divided into three sections. Part One spells out the significance of silent illumination, the cultivation of correct attitudes, and the methods of practice. Part Two includes my commentaries on three specific teachings by Hongzhi, detailing pre- and post-awakening practices. Part Three includes running translations of twenty-five excerpts from Hongzhi's collected writings.

This book is the result of many people's efforts. Special thanks to Julie Myosen Sprott, who transcribed all the talks diligently, and Sandra Fiegehen, who carefully organized the transcripts and gave the first pass at editing the transcripts. She made many editorial suggestions. I would also like to thank Liz Shaw and John Golebiewski at Shambhala as well as the developmental editor, Vanessa Zuisei Goddard. They made this book a reality. Finally, my gratitude to Chan Master Hongzhi, whose silent illumination teaching exemplifies the perfection of the Chan Buddhist path to natural awakening.

I dedicate this book to my teacher, Master Sheng Yen. And to all of you who are holding this book in your hands, may it be your close companion on the path of awakening. May you live freely and share with all beings the wisdom and compassion of silent illumination.

Guo Gu

February 2020

PART ONE
Silent Illumination

1. A Parable for Silent Illumination

THERE IS a wonderful Buddhist parable of a group of blind men who are trying to fathom the nature of an elephant. Each of the men touches a different part of the elephant and then makes a pronouncement about his conclusion. The first man touches its tusk and says that an elephant is like a long, hard white radish. The next man touches its ear and concludes that an elephant is like a winnowing basket. The man who touches its head says that it is like a boulder; the one who touches its trunk says it is like a pillar; the one who touches its belly says that it is like a large urn; the one who touches its tail says that an elephant is like a rope, and so on.[1] Each of the men has his own idea of what an elephant is based on his limited experience.

This parable is from the *Mahaparinirvana-sutra*, and the elephant here is an analogy for buddha-nature, the original and natural awakening within all of us. However, because of our blindness and limited perspective, we only understand and manifest that awakening partially and imperfectly. Thus, we need to find ways, principles, and methods of practice to reveal our true nature.

Buddha-nature, our natural awakened nature, is really another word for silent illumination (*mozhao*). Yet, many misunderstand it as an exclusive meditation method of certain sects within the Chan tradition and say that it was advocated only by Chan master Hongzhi Zhengjue (1091–1157). But silent illumination cannot be claimed by any one tradition within Mahayana Buddhism, and it is not a fixed meditation method. Hongzhi, a child prodigy who at age five had already memorized the four classic books of Confucianism (*Great Learning, The Doctrine of the Mean, Analects*, and *Mencius*) was a gifted teacher. His masterful command of the Chinese language, and his fondness for poetry in particular, is evident in the poetic imagery he used to describe silent illumination, whose qualities are freedom, openness, and clarity. In other words, for him silent illumination was awakening; he never presented it as a "method" or "technique" for meditation practice. In staying true to Hongzhi's description of silent illumination, I present it in this book as natural awakening accessible to everyone, right here and now.

SILENT ILLUMINATION AS NATURAL AWAKENING

Natural awakening is inherent within everyone—it is not something produced through practice. Hongzhi eloquently described it as the "vacant and open field," the "lucid lake," our "original home." The point of Chan practice, then, is to regain our original freedom by clearing away our emotional afflictions and negative habitual patterns (i.e., craving, aversion, and ignorance and our tendency to perpetuate them), the accumulation of which have concealed who we are:

> It [silent illumination] cannot be practiced nor actualized because it is something intrinsically full and complete. Others cannot defile it; it is thoroughly pure to its depth. Precisely at the place where purity is full and complete is where you must open your eyes and recognize it. When illumination is thorough, [self] is relinquished completely—when experiencing is clear, your steps are then solid and grounded.[2]

Elsewhere he states:

> The correct way of practice is to simply sit in stillness and silently investigate; deep down one reaches a state where externally one is no longer swayed by causes and conditions. The mind being empty, it is all-embracing; its luminosity being wondrous, it is precisely apt and impartial.[3]

Chan practice is about investigating our intrinsic awakened nature. It requires us to remove the obscurations—self-attachment and all of its emotional afflictions and negative habitual patterns—that conceal our inherent freedom so we can express it in the midst of daily life.

The transliteration of the Chinese characters Hongzhi used for "investigation" are *jiu* and *can*. Both have the meaning of "partaking," "integrating," and "thoroughly penetrating." Sometimes he combined the word *investiga-*

tion with the term *ti*, which means "embodiment" or "experiencing." For Hongzhi, investigation is not an intellectual process but embodied, actualized, and lived *experiencing*. Thus, while silent illumination as our original awakened nature "is something intrinsically full and complete," we must personally recognize and live it.

"Silence" is the metaphor for the wisdom of emptiness. So are quiescence, formlessness, spaciousness, stillness. These are all Hongzhi's poetic terms for the Mahayana teaching of selflessness. "Illumination" refers to the wondrous activity of this selfless wisdom that, in Buddhism, is none other than compassion. Just as wisdom and compassion are inseparable, so are silence and illumination. They are simply two aspects of our natural awakened buddha-nature within.

Chan teaches that we are already free—we are buddhas. At the same time, we're bogged down by delusion, emotional afflictions, and negative habitual patterns, so we don't realize our freedom. An analogy for this is the room that you occupy right now. The room—its spaciousness—cannot be defined by the furniture contained in it or the presence or absence of people. Nor is the nature of the room affected by its level of cleanliness. Similarly, our buddha-nature is not defined by the presence or absence of our emotional afflictions. Like the spacious room, buddha-nature has always been empty, free of disturbance. At the same time, buddha-nature is not a *thing* apart from emotional afflictions. It is through the vexations of our lives that we realize freedom. By working with our thoughts, feelings, and mental states, we come to realize that we are the dynamic expression of buddha-nature.

The spaciousness or emptiness of the room is the "silence" in silent illumination. The ability of the room to accommodate all sorts of furniture is the "illumination" of silent illumination. Our true mind has no delineating borders, and it has infinite potential; we have the ability to respond to the needs of all beings creatively, immeasurably. Just as space is not the result of our moving the furniture around the room, awakening is not something that we gain from our efforts in "practice." If awakening were gained from practice, then it would be just an additional piece of furniture! Whatever can be gained is also subject to loss. Our buddha-nature has nothing to do with having or lacking, gaining or losing.

Yet, by working with the furniture—fixing the dilapidated pieces, recycling the old ones, and clearing up the clutter—it's more likely that we'll recognize the spaciousness of the room.

The pieces of furniture in our heart-mind are all the ever-changing constructs, narratives, knowledge, and personal experiences. For the purpose of this book, I will use "mind" or "heart-mind" to refer to the workings of our whole being. While our modern sensibilities tell us that body and mind are separate—that there are distinct functions of heart, brain, and mind—in Chan usage, all of these functions are interconnected, synonymous. As for the furniture there is a vitality to their transiency, where nothing is fixed and everything is possible. Furniture can be rearranged and recycled endlessly. We may take a particular piece of furniture as who we are, but there really is no permanent "me" apart from our mental construct of it. There is no self that experiences; there's just moment-to-moment experiencing. The problem is really not with the furniture but with our rigid fixation on it. We are attached to all the things we experience and have allowed them to define, shape, and manipulate us.

When we fully appreciate the natural expression of mind as *experiencing*, all things become alive, fluid, intimately connected to one another. This is the realization of no-self or selflessness. The true nature of our mind is free. This freedom is also our true nature. Thoughts and passing emotions liberate themselves, moment after moment after moment. We don't have to *do* anything to make them disappear. They liberate themselves if we let go of what we're grasping.

Our true nature has infinite potential. It is able to respond to circumstances and the needs of all beings. Expressed as the natural functioning of the mind, our experiencing is both empty and aware. It is able to respond in any and all ways, freely and dynamically, adapting and accommodating to all conditions with effortless flexibility. Just as our eyes see and ears hear—because that is their inherent function—buddha-nature simply *experiences,* moment to moment, because this is its inherent function.

When we are aligned with our buddha-nature, we are like a mirror selflessly reflecting images before it. We respond to complex situations and interact with others effortlessly, and the reason we can function perfectly well without a fixed, rigid sense of self or "experiencer" is because, in reality, there is no such thing and there never was. Self as a permanent entity doesn't exist. In our confusion, we think that the objects of our minds—thoughts and feelings—arise from the "I" that is the subject standing in opposition to the rest of the world.

Our attachment to a fixed sense of I is unnecessary. We can actually function better without it, adapting to changes when faced with obstacles. But when we fixate on this sense of me, I, and mine and inject it into our daily interactions with others, we hinder the natural expression of our buddha-nature as experiencing and cause suffering for ourselves and others. Why? Because it's contrary to how we actually are: free and open, wondrously changing and with great potential. To understand silent illumination is to appreciate our true nature as already free—the natural awakening of who we are.

The reason we don't feel liberated is because we attach to these notions of me, I, and mine. We have taken our thinking and feeling—the objects of experiencing—as who we are. The truth is, if we fill a glass with murky water and then we set the glass down and allow the silt to settle, the water naturally becomes clear. The nature of water is originally clear. It only appears to be temporarily muddied by the silt that it contains. Silent illumination *is* who we are. Clarity has always been present. This is called intrinsic awakening, or what I call natural awakening. Usually, realization of this truth happens suddenly. This is experiential awakening. Water holds the silt particles without resisting their presence or changing its true nature, and the same is true of the heart-mind. If it did not have freedom as its intrinsic nature, how could it liberate itself?

In Buddhism, when intrinsic awakening is experientially realized, it is called selfless wisdom, or *prajna*. Because this wisdom operates freely, without self-referential obstructions, it responds skillfully to the needs of sentient beings. This is called great compassion. Thus, wisdom and compassion are the same thing, just expressed differently. They are inseparable, as are silence and illumination.

THE POETICS OF SILENT ILLUMINATION

Among the various Chan lineages, silent illumination is a shared language for awakening that rests on a playful interdependence of opposites: wisdom and compassion, stillness and activity, quiescence and wakefulness, essence and function. Before the arrival of Buddhism in China, Chinese philosophical traditions often used metaphors to express similar interplays and harmonies between dualities. As a Chinese form of Buddhism, Chan practice is thus naturally expressed through the same poetic language.

Many Chan masters from different lineages used this sort of language.

Consider the words of the famous Linji Chan master, Yuanwu Keqin (1063–1135):

> Directly, your mind should resemble a withered log and a rotten tree stump—like a person who has gone through a great death who no longer breathes. Moment to moment without knowing; instant to instant without abiding. Even a thousand sages cannot call you out [of this state]. Then it may be possible to be like the blossoming of flowers on a withered tree. You would be able to bring forth boundless responses and exhibit the great lively function of kindness and compassion.[4]

The main point of this passage is that only through stilling the mind can we embody the realization of compassion and help sentient beings. The "withered log and a rotten tree stump" point to stillness and silence. Chan master Yuanwu is encouraging practitioners to cultivate the ability to not be swayed by deluded thinking—the furniture of the room. Only then will the mind become truly responsive—like the "blossoming of flowers on a withered tree"—or have the ability to connect with others with genuine kindness and compassion. Compassion is the function of wisdom, just as illumination is the function of silence.

The key to appreciating our natural awakening is in the interplay of silence and illumination, quiescence and wakefulness, stillness and activity. Common to many forms of religious or theological discourse, an "apophatic" approach, or *via negativa,* involves knowing something by affirming that which it is not. For example, emptiness is *not* this or *not* that; it cannot be grasped because it is not a *thing*. These apophatic expressions—and there are plenty in Buddhism—may sound pessimistic or negative but they affirm the inexpressible. Yuanwu here is using metaphorical, not literal, language to harmonize the apophatic expressions with "cataphatic" or *via positiva* language, such as "the blossoming of flowers on a withered tree," to describe both the essence and the function of buddha-nature. The withered tree, representing selfless wisdom, refers to the essence of mind. The blossoming of flowers, representing the natural responsiveness of compassion, refers to the function of mind. This means that only through selfless wisdom could genuine compassion blossom. The contradictory dyad of this metaphor gives it greater impact.

Chan master Dahui Zong'gao (1089–1163) was Yuanwu's disciple. Japanese scholars of Zen typically refer to him as Hongzhi's rival on the basis of their respective differences in their approach to practice: *gong'an* (Jpn. *koan*) versus silent illumination (Jpn. *shikantaza*). Yet the two masters actually speak of practice in similar ways. Dahui writes:

> Those who study the way must be quiet and still their thoughts, feelings, and perceptions during the twelve hours of the day. If there is no particular task that needs to be done, then sit in quiet meditation so that your mind does not become lax, and your body remains motionless. After a while, you will become natural and have a tranquil body and mind, which will put you in proximate accordance with the way.[5]

We are normally so conditioned, and our vision is so clouded by our thoughts, feelings, and perceptions, that the first step to any real cultivation is to learn how to manage these mental processes. To do so, we need to practice meditation and settle the body and mind. Thus, while awakening is our true nature, practice is absolutely necessary. In Hongzhi's words:

> This vacant and open field is intrinsically present from the very beginning. You must purify and wipe away the various deluded conditioning and illusory habits. Naturally, you will arrive at a place that is clear and pure, perfect and bright. Totally empty, without any image, resplendent and outstanding, it does not rely on anything. Only this vastness can illuminate this fundamental reality, as external objects are relinquished.[6]

Indeed, this vacant field—our intrinsic buddha-nature—is empty of hindrances, free of defilements, and originally awakened. This may be a difficult concept for us to understand or accept. If we take a moment to reflect on what is going on with us right at this moment, chances are that what we are most aware of is a constant stream of internal mental chatter or discursive thinking. It is hard to conceptualize, much less experience, an openness of mind in the midst of this constant chatter.

For this reason, Chan practice involves "purifying and wiping away the various deluded conditioning and illusory habits." Thoughts and emotions are only temporary functions of the mind. We can't get caught up with them. We need to expose, embrace, work with, and let go of them. In this process, we regain the most natural state of being: empty yet wakeful; still and aware. Master Yongjia Xuanjue (665–713) describes it like this:

> Wakeful yet quiescent is correct; oblivious and quiescent is wrong. Quiescent yet wakeful is correct; mental scattering in wakefulness is wrong.[7]

Here, Yongjia elucidates the nature of mind as quiescent and wakeful. Even though the mind is quiescent, it is not dull or oblivious; while the mind is wakeful, it is free from scattered thinking. The principle of silent illumination is applicable to practice. Usually, when we are relaxed and still, we fall asleep; when we are awake, our minds are spinning with thoughts. All this is due to habitual tendencies of attaching to different states of mind. So the point is to regain the natural clarity of our mind without being conditioned by thoughts. Being free from conditioning thoughts, our mind becomes wakeful. Not being attached, we do not fall into a state of stupor. I will discuss this principle in more detail and how it is applied to practice in chapter 7.

The point is, even before the emergence of Chan as a tradition, Master Zhiyi (539–598) of the Tiantai school, had already articulated a "perfected teaching" for awakening that is fully embodied in a single moment of awareness as an "ever quiescent, yet luminous" state.[8] Zhiyi described buddha-nature as "quiescent luminosity," and asserted that "all the buddhas in the past, present, and future save themselves and others through precisely this wondrous function of quiescent luminosity."[9] One can find similar expressions of quiescent luminosity in the Huayan or "Flower Garland" commentary tradition (ca. fifth to eighth century).[10] This was also one of the doctrinal schools of Chinese Mahayana Buddhism that flourished before Chan, and many of its teachings were absorbed into this latter school. In short, premodern Chinese Buddhism has had a long tradition of articulating practice and awakening through poetic metaphors.

As a poetic metaphor, silent illumination harmonizes the apophatic and cataphatic ways of expressing our true nature, and this balance provides a principle upon which we can base our practice. If we engage in practice one-sidedly, focusing on either stillness or clarity to the exclusion of the other, we will stray from the path. Mind must be still yet clear, and self must be empty yet engaging with the world. Hongzhi's poetic images are not concepts that we imagine while sitting in meditation. They are pointers that need to be concretely realized in daily life. As Hongzhi says, we must "wipe away the various deluded conditioning and illusory habits" so we can discover "the profound depth of awakening." How do we experience this? How do we concretize this in our practice? This book shows you how.

2. Starting from Where We Are

Chan offers no particular fixed way to practice. The only purpose of practice is to uproot our deep-seated emotional afflictions and negative habitual patterns that conceal our true awakened nature—and at the same time, develop our true potential. Yet, over the centuries, Chan masters have developed numerous skillful means to help people.

Before we discuss the actual practices to realize silent illumination, we need to understand and to develop a conviction regarding our true nature, our buddha-nature. We also need to learn to expose, embrace, and transform the emotional afflictions and negative habitual patterns—the root of which is self-grasping. It is the self, in all of its manifestations, that conceals our true nature. We must begin here to appreciate the teachings of silent illumination so we can live the truth of our intrinsic freedom.

Buddha-Nature

Buddha-nature, our true nature, is simply freedom. It is not a thing. If it were, then it would have a before and an after, it would be subject to birth and death, and would be either permanent or impermanent. Buddha-nature is inconceivable. We, too, are inconceivable. This inconceivability is that right here and right now, *we are free.*

Buddha-nature also means the "potential for buddhahood" in all beings. The word *buddha* means "awake," so this means we all have the potential for awakening. Mahayana scriptures provide the analogy of a womb (Skt. *tathagatagarbha*) within which a buddha resides. *Tathagata* is an epithet for buddha, and *garbha* means "womb" or "storehouse." So *tathagatagarbha* means "buddha in the womb." But *tathagata* literally means "one who has thus come and is thus gone," or simply, "as if come, as if gone." While buddhas may seem to have come and gone, they are neither coming nor going;

they are not born and do not die—birth and death are temporary displays of causes and conditions. The same is true for us. Our true nature is beyond birth and death.

Potential is possibility. If we lacked the potential for awakening, then practice would be useless. An apple seed, under the right conditions, produces an apple tree because the potential already exists in the seed. Cause leads to effect. The effect already exists in the cause. All beings, even murderers, have the same potential for awakening—we are possibilities.

In the Buddha's time there lived a killer named Angulimala.[1] The young man, originally a devout practitioner of another path, was very handsome, and his teacher's wife fell in love with him. She tried to seduce him, but he resisted her. Then she became vengeful and told her husband that Angulimala had tried to seduce her. The teacher believed her and, even though Angulimala was a good student, decided that he had to get rid of him. He told his student that he was going to give him a "secret teaching," but first he asked him to kill 1,000 people and bring him their fingers. Angulimala was reluctant to do so, but the teacher insisted that he must prove himself capable of learning the greatest teaching of all. In fact, his plan was to get Angulimala killed in the process.

Angulimala finally decided to comply with his teacher's instruction and, being a strong young man, succeeded in killing 999 people. In that frenzy of killing, he lost his mind. (I'm sure we have all had the experience of really getting into something and losing our way.) When Angulimala had one last victim to kill, he saw the Buddha coming down the road. Angulimala ran toward the Buddha with his sword with the intent to kill his last victim and complete his task. The Buddha was walking slowly and it seemed Angulimala would have no difficulty finishing him off, but the young man found that he could not catch up to the master, even though the Buddha appeared to not be moving at all. Angulimala finally called out to the Buddha in frustration, "Stop!" The Buddha replied, "Angulimala, I have already stopped for the sake of all beings; it is *you* who have not stopped." Angulimala was so moved that he abandoned his ways and became a monk under Shakyamuni. Soon, he became an arhat, a liberated person, and entered nirvana.

We may think that Angulimala was born with buddha-nature but somehow lost it when he became deluded by his actions. Some people believe that all children are born "innocent" but lose that inherent innocence through the conditioning of culture and family or through the pain and suffering caused by their experience. Likewise, we might think that it's possible to lose our buddha-nature, but this interpretation is inaccurate. Buddha-nature *is* the nature of emptiness. It can take the form of a child and it can also manifest as an Angulimala who does horrible things as a result of certain causes and conditions. But, amid delusion and conditioning, buddha-nature is never lost.

In the face of all the difficulties that we experience, each one of us tries to live the best way we can, responding to whatever conditions we find ourselves in. Those who are suffering and harming others are simply giving form to the workings of buddha-nature in delusion. When we're awakened, buddha-nature expresses itself as wisdom; when we're deluded, it appears as ignorance. We must awaken to who we are in order to embody the truth of our buddha-nature amid the complexities of life.

We can't recognize buddha-nature because we are so steeped in our created world of dualities. We perpetuate notions of good and evil, gaining and losing, success and failure, victim and perpetrator—all of which revolve around the central vantage point of me, I, and mine. It is precisely due to this self-referential polarization that we suffer and inflict the same suffering on others. We can free ourselves from this cycle by not confusing emotional afflictions with our true nature (by not confusing the furniture with the spaciousness of the room). When we free ourselves in this way, we allow the buddha-nature of those around us to also manifest. Through our understanding, we can engage with all beings in such a way as to help them bring out their own wisdom and compassion. To do all this, we must engage in practice.

As my teacher once said, "People who experience personal suffering and undergo calamities and disasters are all great bodhisattvas." Why should we reduce them to pitiable victims? Conversely, why should we see those who inflict harm as perpetrators? Is it possible that they are themselves victims in some way? Moreover, do their actions possibly reflect our own tendencies to some extent? Could we see them as bodhisattvas and let them draw out our compassion for ourselves and them, and therefore change the world? What is unjust and wrong must be corrected. But we can do so with wisdom and compassion for ourselves and others. All beings, including us, are suffering in a world of oppositions. Yet, in this suffering, there is also buddha-nature and awakening.

Buddha-nature is not something we've lost, but it is present right here and now. It's not a primordial state that we have to get back to. If we think like this, then we will create an opposition of past and present. We might even blame others for why we've lost it in the first place. We may see ourselves as the victims of our history, our culture, our education system, and so forth—all the things that have made us "lose" our true nature. Buddha-nature exists in all, right here and right now. It is up to us to actualize it.

Buddha-nature manifests in all situations and at all times. It is empty of fixations but full of possibilities; it can be empty of delusions but full of compassion. This is the correct understanding. Whatever difficulties we may face, it's all good—IAG, as I like to say. We practice engaging with all sentient beings so as to free all from suffering.

THE SELF

In delusion, buddha-nature appears as self. Yet, originally there is no self. It only appears as such because we attach to it the sense of me, I, and mine, and all the objects that we hold on to. Self is the result of grasping. Cultivation begins with exposing, embracing, transforming, and letting go of self-referential grasping so we can realize the full potential of buddha-nature as wisdom and compassion. Only then will we be able to truly live, love, and bring to fulfillment who we truly are.

For most of us, attachment to our thoughts and feelings—our inner monologues—defines who we are. They are all that we've ever known about ourselves. We're completely entwined with them, and we find it difficult to understand that we are more than just our narratives, likes and dislikes—that we are originally free. Buddhist teachings point to the moment-to-moment emergence of phenomena in our minds—sensations, conceptions—and give these mental phenomena the general label of "mental continuum." This mental continuum is experienced at different levels. At the very coarse level, our experience is that of a "self." We have a sense that we are *here*, separate from what we see *there*. Even when we use a method of meditation, we feel we're sitting, using a method, and thoughts come and go, invading our mental continuum. There seems to be an "I" that's sitting and experiencing "my" thoughts. This "I" feels like a solid reference point, a center through which we experience everything that's not this center.

For example, as you read these words, you probably see their visual form and hear the internal speech they elicit as you read them. You also feel the sensations in your body as you read and are aware of the one who is witnessing all these things. In other words, there's you and then all the things you are experiencing. On this very superficial level, you feel there's a mind containing all these objects, and there is someone who possesses this mind, cluttered as it sometimes is. Even the internally generated thoughts are somehow objectively experienced by the "me" of you. You feel you are the subjective experiencer, and you have a sense of "I" that is in opposition to the world out there.

This sense of "I" is a byproduct of the natural functioning of the brain's neurological wiring, which generates a sense of self that helps us to navigate the world. This subjectivity—this sense of a separate self—is not where the problem lies. Subjectivity is the natural function of the brain. The problem lies with our deep-seated attachment to this me, I, and mine and the discursive thinking that reifies it into a *thing*. So it's our attachment to this mental construction that leads us astray from our true nature. Chan teaches that this nature is intrinsically free from these fragmented, random mental activities that come and go, rise and perish. That's their nature: they liberate themselves, instant by instant, as they come and go.

That said, no-self is not a concept that we need to take on faith, nor is it a particular belief system that we have to accept unreservedly. It is simply the way things are. Even neuroscientists tell us that our "self" is just patterns of neuro-synaptic firings that change continuously. When we fixate on something that doesn't exist, we make erroneous choices and experience the consequences: suffering.

One way to realize this selfless freedom, this fluid nature, is to apply ourselves to meditation. As we practice meditation, the mind starts to become more calm, concentrated, and clear. As our discursive thinking starts to subside, the mind naturally becomes focused on one thing—the method of meditation itself. As we progress, a subtler level of experience begins to manifest moment to moment. I call this "freshness." There's only the *experiencing* itself, which is vibrant, not abiding anywhere, and lacks words or language to describe it.

At this subtle level, while we're meditating, we might hear the sound of an automobile going by, but its passing doesn't leave any trace on our minds. In each moment, we perceive with freshness, and when the object disappears, our perception vanishes with it. We continue with our meditation.

If we persist in the practice, all of our fragmented and scattered thoughts are reduced to a single point—the present moment—and going further, even our last bit of attachment to the present may suddenly vanish. When this happens, self-grasping disappears, leaving us with just experiencing—without self. Buddha-nature manifests. This vivid experiencing, wakeful and focused, is liberating.

That said, our persistence in genuine practice is dependent on our ability to work with the undercurrent feeling tones—all the subtle thoughts—that shape our everyday experience. In the next chapter I focus exclusively on this important topic as a foundation for appreciating silent illumination.

3. The Underlying Feeling Tones

To be free, we must know what we should be free of. Ordinarily, our minds are cluttered with the thoughts and feelings of everyday living. Sometimes these thoughts are not fully formed concepts but are simply underlying feeling tones. Most people are unaware of these feeling tones, yet, it is precisely these feelings that shape our choices, reasoning, experience, and judgment. So we have to learn to recognize them and work with them by cultivating particular attitudes.

In practice, we need to develop an awareness of the overall tone of our internal states. By helping us to clear out the clutter in our minds, meditation exposes these hidden internal states so that we can do something about them. Is this clearing itself awakening? No. It is simply practice, and self-grasping may still be present.

In the Yogachara or "Consciousness-Only" school of Buddhism, the underlying feeling tones are understood as "mental factors."[1] At any given moment, in waking or sleeping life, there is always a mental factor present. If, for example, the mental factor of restlessness is present in your mind, then no matter how you meditate, you will not be able to settle down. I call these mental factors "underlying feeling tones"—attitudes or moods we need to work with because they are often obstructive or negative. They can color our experience and prevent us from seeing things as they truly are. On the other hand, if we become aware of these feeling tones and learn to cultivate the right attitude toward them, then we will feel more grounded. Our wandering thoughts will decrease, and we can become more focused in meditation and life.

Chan master Hongzhi refers to feeling tones as "dustlike intentions" and "concerns" that conceal the original bright mirror-mind of natural awakening. Hongzhi teaches that we have to recognize that there is nothing outside ourselves. If we expose and loosen our grasp on these feeling tones, we will not be affected by the objects of our experiencing either, because we no longer experience subject and object as separate, even when we fully engage with the world:

> Silent and still, abiding in itself, this suchness is apart from conditioning. Its luminosity is vast and spacious, without any dust—directly, [delusion] is thoroughly relinquished. Arriving at this fundamental place, you realize that it is not something newly acquired today.... Though it is like this, it must be actualized. To actualize it in this moment is to simply not allow a single thing to arise, a single speck of dust to cover it ... be spaciousness and completely clear ... and don't engage with dustlike intentions; dissolve your concerns. Just take a backward step and open your grasping hands.[2]

The subtle intentions and concerns are the undercurrents of our interior experience that shape our choices and perceptions. We have to expose them and free ourselves from their shackles. We need to know that nothing defines us, binds us.

Once we have exposed negative feeling tones, we can foster correct attitudes that resonate with our original freedom. Many of our subtle tendencies are hidden from our awareness. If we are unaware of what's going on inside us, simply practicing seated meditation won't take us too far along the road to liberation. This is why many practitioners, after years of meditation, wonder why it is that they are still vexed by the same people and events in their lives. How can it be that in seated meditation they're able to gain peace, but in the busyness of life they are basically the same people? If we don't expose the subtle tendencies that govern the way we practice and, in turn, cultivate correct attitudes, we inevitably perpetuate separateness, opposition, and self-referential thinking. These subtle undercurrent tendencies manifest as the attitudes we have toward life. We need to expose them and cultivate the right attitudes to bring out our wisdom and compassion.

From a Buddhist perspective, the distinction between thoughts and feeling tones is that thoughts are fully formed concepts, while the feeling tones are subtle intentions, perceptions, or moods, which are subtle thoughts. Whether we realize it or not, there are millions of subtle feeling tones that shape our experience in any given situation. We're just not aware of them. There is no clear-cut difference between thoughts and feelings. Yet, we make a clear divide between them, which then shapes the way we articulate our inner experience and even understand Buddhism. For example, many people read the Buddhist literature on the importance of having correct "view," and they interpret it as some kind of knowledge or understanding—in other words, as correct thought. This is only partially correct. In Buddhism, thoughts and feelings are inseparable. If we can cultivate wholesome attitudes, we would naturally have correct understanding of things. Therefore, I emphasize cultivating correct attitudes and being more aware of subtle feeling tones.

In order to become aware of undercurrent feeling tones, we have to train ourselves to experience them. The more immersed in our inner states we are, the more experienced we become, and the more we're able to navigate them and become skillful practitioners.

We have to cultivate some important attitudes in our practice. These attitudes should be cultivated in all aspects of our lives, beyond mere sitting meditation. In the remainder of this and the next chapters, I list some of these important attitudes. It is up to each of us to explore them one by one, then together, to see their interconnections and also the ways they affect our inner experience. Cultivating correct attitudes transforms the way we carry ourselves, relate to others, and engage with the world. In this way, everything becomes our path. Life becomes practice, so we can foster the necessary prerequisites to realizing silent illumination.

How to Cultivate Right Attitudes

We can cultivate right attitudes through a fourfold process of exposing, embracing, transforming, and letting go. When practitioners come across the familiar Buddhist teaching of non-grasping, they think that they have to let go of everything, that this is something they can do right away, and that once they've done so, everything will be fine. The truth is, we have to first see what it is that we have to let go of. We have to expose our subtle emotional afflictions and negative habits. In exposing them, we may recognize that they have been part of us for a long time; that there is history behind our behaviors. They may be part of our defense mechanisms and survival skills. So, we have to accept them. Only when we accept them will we be able to take responsibility for and work through them. Then we will no longer be under their influence. This is letting go of them.

This is a long process, and it is not linear but circular. The more we're able to see, the more we need to embrace. The more we embrace and let our feelings come through us, the more we are able to expose the deeper layers of our habits. The more we work through them, the more we are able to let go and accept ourselves. In time we become freer. This letting go is actually the easiest part of the process because it happens naturally and suddenly, but we must first do our preparatory work. We cannot anticipate when these habitual tendencies will release themselves, and we cannot will it to happen. Practice is a lifetime process that brings out the best in us.

CONTENTMENT

The first attitude we have to cultivate is the feeling of contentment. Contentment counters and overrides our constant tendency to grasp and chase after things. Contentment has the flavor of being at ease—grasping nothing, lacking nothing. It is being open and leisurely. In this state, we don't make anything into a big deal, while at the same time we engage with the freshness of each moment. Cultivating an attitude of contentment is engaging with and yet not grasping at causes and conditions.

We are swayed by causes and conditions when we feel a sense of lack and when grasping is present. We inevitably get sucked into the vortex of grasping and rejecting, having and lacking. These polarities bring up all sorts of other issues, such as trying to escape from who we are or, alternately, trying desperately to be someone we're not.

There is no formulaic way to cultivate contentment or non-grasping. We need to personally explore the flavor of contentment and digest this feeling little by little, becoming familiar with it in our lives. We can't just force this attitude on ourselves and expect to be able to plow through all of our problems. Contentment is not a mere concept. We need to appreciate the depth of what it means to be content. It is not just being disinterested or detached from everything.

When we're content, we appreciate what we have, and we are able to engage fully with whatever may arise. There's a freshness to it. With contentment, we're able to avail ourselves openly of everything, without rejecting anything. In this process, there may be pain and grief. But we are cultivating the ability to feel fully, to be present to whatever arises without judgment. Allowing such feelings to move through us will make us stronger. We are incredibly resilient. Our hearts and minds will eventually accept and release whatever comes through us.

To do this, we have to be in tune with the body and anchor ourselves in it. Contentment resides in the heart, and it has an associated bodily component. The easiest way to become familiar with contentment is to physically relax the body. We relax from the crown of the head to the toes, section by section. We relax the skin, pores, muscles, tendons. This means actually feeling different areas of our bodies. Most people are so out of tune with their bodies that they don't really know how to relax or what their bodies feel, so this requires practice.

In chapter 5, I discuss this method of relaxation fully, but for now the important thing to know is that as you explore relaxing your body during meditation, as you become physically and emotionally familiar with it, you will then be able to tune in to contentment. The more familiar you are with contentment, the more likely you will be able to apply it to your daily life. Responding to changing conditions, you will have no need to solidify your viewpoints, narratives, and emotional afflictions.

Being in tune with bodily feelings of contentment and non-grasping releases physical pain. For example, sometimes after long hours of sitting meditation we experience waves of bodily pain and an attitude of repulsion sets in—naturally, we want to escape the pain. If we are oblivious to the subtle undertone of repulsion, the pain becomes more acute and intractable. Soon our whole body is burning up. However, when we expose what is happening within us, we can detect whether we are feeling aversion. Perhaps we are bolstering this discomfort with stories and images. Is there an underlying tone of fear? When aversion is present, pain becomes exaggerated. So if any of these negative feelings are present, we need to first expose our attitude and then relax the body physically. Only then will it become easier to soften our negative feelings and to release them. Actually, the exposing and relaxing are, in themselves, a way of working with these negative feelings. And this work will naturally bring about a shift in our attitude toward physical discomfort. Not only does our threshold for it increase; the pain itself actually becomes bearable. But if we can't even recognize how we're feeling and how it is shaping our actual experience, how can we let go of negative mental states?

Contentment is traditionally expressed in Chan as non-grasping. In the *Platform Scripture*, Master Huineng (638–713) provides three principles to deal with it: no-thought, no-form, and non-abiding. These three principles are antidotes to our grasping of our inner world, outer relations, and identity.

In order to appreciate these three principles, we need to recognize grasping as a deep-seated feeling tone. It's a sense of lack, a thirst for some *thing*. Of course, being discontented can bring about change for the better in our lives, but here I'm referring to a habit of possessiveness, which arises from self-grasping.

Huineng says:

> Good friends, since the past this teaching of ours has first taken no-thought as its principle, no-form as its essence, and non-abiding as its foundation. No-thought means to be without "thought" in the midst of thinking. No-form is to transcend form within the context of forms and appearances. Non-abiding is your fundamental nature . . . all worldly things are empty.[3]

Thoughts, feelings, and narratives are what we grasp internally. Form is what we grasp externally, and this can include our bodies, objects, environment, status, wealth, and appearances. None of these objects of grasping are in and of themselves bad. Sometimes they are needed to help us navigate through life and improve our circumstances. However, when our grasping is driven by possessiveness and obsession, it brings about suffering for ourselves and others. Non-abiding is just a Chan way of saying non-grasping. Everything is fluid, changing, open to opportunities. This is how things—including ourselves—are. Nothing is fixed, rigid. How can anything be grasped?

Grasping and rejecting are always based on our self-referential obsessions. If we are captivated or repulsed by whatever comes up in our practice, then it gains power over us, and the problem becomes worse. When difficulties arise, it is important to see them clearly, accept them, work with them, and let them go. The true nature of things is non-abiding, fresh, and dynamic. Relating to our feelings and thoughts through grasping and rejecting ruins everything. If we grasp at them, then we're going against their nature. We suffer, and probably cause everyone around us to suffer. When we grasp and reject, we're ultimately concerned with me, I, and mine. We're thinking self-referentially.

The opposite of thinking, grasping, and abiding is contentment, and it's the most important of all attitudes to cultivate in order to see our inner experiences and outer relations as our true nature.

No-Thought

How do we relate to our inner experience? In the above *Platform Scripture* passage, "no-thought" does not mean cutting off thinking—it means there is no fixation with regard to the free flow of our thinking. We don't need to reify or solidify what we experience into *my* thoughts, *my* feelings. If self-grasping is present, then thoughts don't flow. When we suffer, we are caught in the middle of the stories that we're fabricating, and, in this way, we prolong that suffering.

Ordinarily, our happiness is completely dependent on thoughts, narratives, concepts, and words. So if we have negative, self-disparaging thoughts and we automatically identify with them, then we will feel very unhappy. If someone praises us, and we identify with that, then we will feel very happy. This is quite normal. Unfortunately, when we're tethered to our thoughts, we actually lose our autonomy. Like a puppet, we are tied up by the strings of our thoughts—completely at the mercy of our narratives. The problem is not with thoughts. The problem is the strings that tie us to those thoughts: our grasping and rejecting.

Here, thought has two levels of meaning. The first refers to our mental activity—our brain's natural ability to think, symbolize, conceptualize, cognize, and perceive. The second level refers to our fixation on our own constructs, notions, and story lines—in other words, our tendency to reify ideas and feelings into discrete realities—into *things*. There is no problem with our natural ability to think, imagine, and so on. The problem is when we start to solidify our thoughts and feelings into fixed notions of me, I, and mine.

To practice contentment, we have to first expose our sense of lack or our need to possess something. Don't identify with these subtle feeling tones. At the same time, don't block them either. There are reasons why we feel and think the way we do. Our thoughts and feelings reveal something about us. Recognizing them as they arise and not grasping or rejecting them is itself a way to own and embrace them. When we can allow ourselves to be with them, we can start to work with them, to work through them, and to let go of them, which means they no longer have a strong hold over us.

We generally believe that the way we think about ourselves *is* how we actually are. We cannot distinguish between our thoughts and the reality of who we are. Moreover, we tend to treat ourselves according to whatever subtle feelings we happen to have at the moment. If we're feeling negative, we don't see anything good about ourselves. When we're in a good mood, even a shortcoming is adorable. This projection happens so quickly that we don't usually recognize it. But this subtle feeling is what the passage above calls "thought." So when you feel something within, recognize it but don't reify, identify, and solidify it into *thing*. Definitely don't build a whole narrative around it. This is the meaning of practicing "no-thought" amid thoughts. It's learning to have a healthier relationship with our thoughts, instead of being conditioned by them.

Sometimes we build a whole narrative around some spiritual experiences we've had. This is another way we reify the natural flow of thoughts. When we have powerful experiences and want a teacher to verify it as awakening, then this very need for verification is a form of self-grasping. If a person has "woken up" from a dream, why would they need verification from someone else? Why would there be a need to announce to the world that they've woken up?

The free flow of our minds is the wonderful, dynamic activity of our creativity and intellect. There's no need to stop thoughts. At the same time, it is necessary to develop the ability to be free from thoughts. One way to do that is to cultivate, through meditation, the ability to bring the mind from a scattered state to a concentrated state, and from the concentrated state to a unified state, and then to free our grasping of even the unified state—the place where subject and object merge. I will return to this point in chapter 5 when I speak about meditation.

No-Form

No-form is a teaching on how to relate to the external world. Ordinarily, we grasp appearances and characteristics as discrete *things*. But there's really not a single thing—nothing is fixed. There is no fixed objective reality. "To transcend form within the context of forms" is a teaching on not denying or divorcing ourselves from form, but allowing all appearances and characteristics to be without us contaminating them with our projections, ideas, or feelings. We must engage with the world while, at the same time, we have no vexations about it. When there's room for improvement, we try our best to improve the world of form. When things need to change, we make the change. But emotional afflictions only lead to more vexations. They can contaminate and even ruin everything we see, hear, smell, taste, and touch.

How do we contaminate forms and appearances? We defile them by attaching to them, reifying them as things "out there." When we make everything into a *thing*, everything we touch can become a problem. For example, I have a student who makes a big deal out of everything. Every task she takes on, however small, she makes into a "thing," and it's always a struggle, always complicated, because she overthinks things. I have another student, and for him everything he encounters is *not* a big deal. Yet, because he feels it is not a big deal, all sorts of unexpected things come up and he makes mistakes. Still, that doesn't really bother him. Both attitudes are problematic. Both follow their own ideas about things "out there." Both have contaminated the "form" with their own habit tendencies. This is not the meaning of no-form: engage with forms and appearances, do what is appropriate, but without grasping onto a fixed way of doing things. No-form also applies to meditation practice. The *Platform Scripture* states:

> "Good friends, what is 'meditative concentration' [i.e., *chan ding*]? Externally, to transcend characteristics is meditation [or *chan*]. Internally, to be undisturbed is called concentration [or *ding*]."[4]

This passage says that meditation means to not be externally swayed by causes and conditions, and not to be internally disturbed by our own thoughts and feelings. But to do this, we have to first become aware of what's going on inside us—how we're projecting our own standards, ideals, and expectations onto the world of form. So no-thought is intimately connected to no-form. How we feel inside is how we relate to others outside. We externalize our internal habits.

One of the most common forms of conditioning in meditation is to fall asleep when we relax. Trying to be clear, we tense up and give rise to wandering thoughts. To practice no-form in terms of seated meditation means to stay relaxed but wakeful, clear but without wandering thoughts. I will return to this point when I discuss meditation practice.

Whether in daily life or in meditation, the world of form operates through causes and conditions. All appearances are fluid. How, then, do we work with the changing appearances of form? How do we live in the world of causes and conditions? What about injustice, discrimination, wrongdoing? Of course, the wrongs of the world must be corrected. Each thing is exactly how it's supposed to be through the workings of causes and conditions.

This means we need to engage with causes and conditions if we are to better the world. Causes and conditions are about relationships. In working with various relationships, we have to recognize, adapt, wait, and create the right causes and conditions for change. Otherwise, emotional afflictions will follow our every move.

Working with causes and conditions also includes relating people. If we want peace and harmony, we must recognize or expose our discriminations. For example, if you interact with people different from you and become vexed, then that's the indicator that you're attached to some kind of form. In our own discrimination and xenophobia—whether conscious or not—we assume that our own perception of the world and of people is the standard of truth. Believing that certain people are different from us, we shun them. Yet evidence shows that it is precisely when we have more interactions across diverse groups of people that we have more ideas, more productivity, and tolerance. Large cities with the highest number of immigrants have the highest level of open-mindedness. But the reverse is also true. So in order to advance peace, harmony, and prosperity, we must also adapt or change our viewpoint, and create more cross-cultural exchange programs, enable the circulation of different ideas, and have a willingness to connect with others in order to appreciate the benefits of diversity. This is formless practice, as it relates to causes and conditions.

A student suggested to me that I lead intensive Chan retreats for people of color. I thought that was a good idea. People of color may feel more comfortable practicing with one another; they may share similar life narratives and identity. But I said to her that while there are benefits, there is also the risk of inadvertently advocating segregation and divisiveness. In our current political climate where divisiveness seems to be the norm, what I try to do is to promote interracial interaction. This is part of recognizing causes and conditions. I do encourage people of color to come together, mingling with each other, sharing their uniquely personal experiences with others. This is adapting and creating the proper causes and conditions to facilitate practice. But ultimately, the point is to bring people of all colors together, so no one is left out.

To recognize, adapt, wait, and create the right causes and conditions is practice. There's no room for self-centeredness. We have to recognize the workings of causes and conditions, adapt and wait for the opportunities, and create the right conditions for change. The right timing is also important. Change occurs with time. Sometimes only the right person or people can cause changes.

The *Platform Scripture*'s phrase, "to transcend form within the context of forms," can be applied to our own lives and to our sociopolitical life. We have to recognize, to adapt, to wait, and to create the conditions of our lives. In this process, if we attach to our own ideas—whether we're pro change or pro status quo—the outcome may be more divisiveness. But if we make our sociopolitical life part of our practice, free up our ideological fixations, recognize and work with causes and conditions, we learn to be free amid the myriad of forms.

To not attach to form we must practice no-thought, which means being more open to new ideas and less rigid about our own opinions. When we expose our own subtle fixation to thoughts and ideas, we will be able to work with form. If we're thinking that the world out there is unjust, without seeing what's going on inside us, then we may be simply contaminating the world of form with our own attachments.

Non-Abiding

Non-abiding is relating to ourselves and others in an open and receptive way, where we allow everything to flow and recognize that each moment is alive, vibrant, filled with infinite possibilities. This is actually the nature of experiencing, the workings of buddha-nature, and the direct expression of natural awakening. For this reason, "non-abiding is your fundamental nature," as Huineng said. It is who we are, free from the internal shackles of thoughts and feelings and the external conditioning of form.

We want things to stay the same because it gives us a sense of security and control. But nothing stays the same. When we embrace change, we become vulnerable, and this vulnerability is true courage. There is strength in being okay with a loss of control, with unpredictability and potential loss. In truth, nothing can break us. We as humans are so resilient. It is only when we try to control and hold on to things that we feel broken. The reverse is also true: when we experience loss, we desperately try to control. This is because deep inside we feel broken, so we try to fix ourselves. We resist how things really are. But if we embrace our vulnerability, tap into who we truly are, and align with non-abiding, whatever difficulties we face will eventually be integrated within us and will be resolved.

How do we cultivate non-abiding? By having the courage to be vulnerable. By engaging with ourselves and the world without fighting everything. There's always going to be opposition when we fixate on ideas about me, I, and mine. But we can respond to the world without injecting a sense of "self" into our decisions, views, and endeavors. This means our own ideas about gain and loss, benefit and harm, do not block our decisions and experiences. Instead, we consider what is needed depending on the circumstances.

The difficulties we face in life are indicators of where we are stuck. We must allow ourselves to be open to our underlying feelings and allow them to come through without judging ourselves. Then we can be content and relax our grasping tendencies. We are then able to face causes and conditions and work with them. In non-opposition and openness, everything eventually works out within us.

We have to cultivate an attitude of contentment, of harmonizing our feelings, and both of these in combination with the three teachings above from the *Platform Scripture*. When we do this, our hearts and minds will be open and integrated.

4. Supporting Attitudes to Cultivate

In the last chapter we looked at the importance of contentment. Here we'll consider several additional attitudes that are beneficial to cultivate.

Interest

Interest is an important attitude that we should cultivate in our lives. Interest has the quality of engagement, but it is not controlling. It is fascination without interference. A good analogy for noninterference is that of a mother sitting in a room with her toddler, letting the toddler play while she knits. In this way, she is present with the child but doesn't have to fixate her gaze on them or control their every move. Similarly, in our meditation we're engaged with a method but we're not tensely focused on it. Our attitude is contentment yet with interest. If we're tense or controlling, then even if we have the best method in the world, we're not going to be able to use it because our minds will be agitated.

Think of the analogy of a relaxed cat watching a mouse hole. The cat is not terribly intense when watching a mouse hole, but it is focused. It's relaxed, but ready at any moment to pounce on a mouse if it comes out of the hole. It's not tense, but ready and awake. Its mere presence, sitting awake in front of the mouse hole, is enough to scare the mice. They dare not come out because they know that the cat is there. If you adopt this kind of wakeful interest, your wandering thoughts are subdued because the mind is at once relaxed, yet focused and watchful.

Noninterference does not mean disinterest, however. When I was in college, I lived in New York City above a Buddhist temple that had a lazy temple cat. The temple also had mice—lots of them—but the cat never did anything to them. You might say that the cat was too compassionate because he didn't kill any of the mice. But I think it was simply disinterested. The mice would walk across the room scavenging for food and crumbs as we ate our dinner, and the cat would just lie there, sleeping.

In practice, you have to be interested. You can't be like the disinterested, lazy temple cat. You have to develop a clear, watchful mind with which you experience the method, whatever that may be. The mice—your scattered thoughts—wander. If you don't do anything about them, they will continue ceaselessly.

If you're meditating on the sensations of the breath while cultivating an attitude of interest, then every breath is fascinating and includes new sensations. This interest keeps you on the method. There's no need to get rid of wandering thoughts—just be more interested in your method. This attitude of interest has a freshness to it. If your mind is interested—vibrant and wakeful—you won't take your method for granted, believing that you already know how to do it. Every moment is fresh, and you can engage with it fully. This is the right attitude of interest.

The attitude of interest works together with contentment. Thus, I am not saying we just "accept what is." When you say something "is," you have already labeled it and made a decision to accept it. Rather, let whatever arises in meditation be what it is, but don't get involved in judging or discriminating thoughts. Interest should not take you off the trail of the method so that you become interested in everything that arises during meditation. That is just being scattered. Developing interest refers to being one with whatever you may be doing, whether it's the method of your practice or being present for a person.

We might view our method as something with which we have a relationship. If disinterest is our attitude when we're with someone, how will our attitude affect the relationship? It certainly will not be good for us or the other person. Try examining yourself when you are in that drowsy or hazy state and see what your attitude is. Be honest with yourself. See yourself and your method as relationship partners. Are you being a good partner or are you being a pain—grasping, rejecting, seeking, abandoning? Is your interest in your partner half-hearted or even lacking? A good partner is attentive and accepting, aware of the shortcomings of the other but willing to work with them.

If we bring an attitude of disinterest to our meditation practice, then we are going to get nowhere. The more we practice with a negative or disinterested attitude, the more we will strengthen a psychosomatic pattern in our meditation—for example, every time we sit, fifteen or twenty minutes into the sitting, we become drowsy.

The body acquires muscle memory for a particular task—playing the piano, for example—over time. The pianist just looks at the music score and their hands know where to place themselves on the keyboard. Similarly, whatever kind of neurobiological habit patterns we've established over successive sittings will repeat themselves automatically every time we practice. If we create negative patterns, we will find it very difficult to undo them.

The process of meditation practice is not simply a mental one. In the body, our patterns of brain activity and our neurological and hormonal levels change according to levels of concentration. In general, the mind needs engagement with an object or some kind of sensory stimulation in order to sustain attention. So practicing meditation is a balancing act. We don't want to attach ourselves to an object, but we do want to stay awake. That is where our attitude of interest is of great importance. If we sincerely care about our practice, if we are sensitive and interested in our method, then we will be creating good habits, and we will avoid falling into bad ones.

We have to know when to advance, when to retreat, when to sharpen the mind, and when to relax when we work with our method. It's a relationship. There is no one fixed way; a one-trick pony approach won't cut it. This is how to be skillful in practice. Approaches to meditation practice are not mechanical. We have to approach our practice with finesse, adapting to the changing conditions. We may be applying our method diligently and may have developed clarity, but if there is the slightest shift in our undercurrent feeling toward disinterest, then slowly we will lose concentration. If there is a taint of annoyance or resistance toward wandering thoughts as an underlying feeling tone, then we will have more wandering thoughts. Gradually our minds will become agitated without us even knowing it.

If we take care of our meditation practice and develop great interest in it, we will take care of our lives the same way. If we recognize the attitude that we bring to practice and, by extension, our lives, then we will have an opportunity to transform it. Our relationships improve. Life becomes easier. In the process, we serve others more skillfully. If our attitude is one of disinterest, however subtle, we can recognize and replace it with acceptance, even love or gratitude. We don't need to be slaves to the habit tendencies that lie beneath the surface of our mental lives. If we practice with an attitude of interest, then with every difficulty that we experience, every obstruction, we will find it easier to change for the better. With interest, we will be able to give rise to great confidence and steadfast determination.

CONFIDENCE

Confidence is an important prerequisite for Chan practice. The word *confidence* in Buddhism also includes other shades of meaning, such as belief, faith, conviction, and trust. All of these qualities are based on experience; they are not based on blind belief. If they're not grounded in personal experience, they will not hold up against the challenges of life and practice. Only experience fosters genuine confidence. On the basis of personal experience, self-confidence develops and, on the basis of self-confidence, confidence in the dharma develops. On the basis of confidence in the dharma, trust in the teacher develops. The teacher represents the sangha, and the Buddha is the origin of dharma. Thus, faith and confidence in the efficacy of the Three Jewels of Buddha, Dharma, and Sangha is established through practice.

Unlike worldly accomplishments, genuine transformative practice and experience rarely come from reason or knowledge. For example, if a meditator is able to ease or even forget about leg pain because they received proper instructions for meditating on pain, they will naturally develop confidence in themselves and their meditation practice. If a person just reads about meditating on pain, this experience is not actually going to alleviate that pain. However reasonable the method may sound, we have to practice it before we can form any opinion about its efficacy.

Chan practitioners must have confidence in buddha-nature, our intrinsic freedom, but this confidence is not something we can rationalize. I've met Zen practitioners who, in meditation, bring forth this faith in "just sitting" as an expression of awakening or buddha-nature. It *is* an expression of buddha-nature, but, when I inquire further about it, I find that what they're doing is *thinking* about faith and conviction in buddha-nature while they sit. They are engaging in a monologue to remind themselves about their faith and conviction. This is not having confidence in buddha-nature. Confidence is not thinking. It is a conviction that arises from experience. To develop confidence, we need to cultivate correct attitudes and use the methods of practice. When we practice with contentment and interest and move away from self-reference, conviction in our freedom naturally grows. The less self-centered we are, the more our conviction grows.

Confidence builds incrementally, within the range of our abilities. If you just started learning about meditation, you can't say, "I'm going to sit in meditation unmoving until I reach full awakening, like the Buddha." If you try to do this, you're going to be disappointed. Please don't set yourself up for defeat. While the motivation is worthy of praise, you have to be realistic. On the other hand, if you say, "I vow not to stray off the method for five or ten minutes of sitting," then maybe that is more reasonable. You may not be able to do it right away or all the time, but when you do you will develop confidence not only in yourself but also in your method, the practice. When people experience some benefit from practice, they begin to have faith in it.

Confidence is an attitude built on experience. It must be cultivated, so we must take action to cultivate it and let our personal experience deepen it. Confidence is a virtue we all have, but we have to engage in practice to develop it. For beginners in meditation, it is helpful to set a time every day for ten to fifteen minutes of sitting. Don't try to sit for too long at first but gradually, over a period of a few months, increase the time to half an hour. As you experience the benefits of your practice, you will be more likely to want to meditate.

In order to cultivate self-confidence, we need to first learn to follow through on our intentions with small tasks. Don't set grand projects that are impossible to accomplish. If we do things incrementally and accomplish them, we can move ourselves from "I can't" to "I can."

I have a student who hoards a lot of stuff. She knows that she should clean up her home but it's overwhelming—everything means so much to her. I told her, "Start with one area at a time—the stairs to the second floor, for example." Her stairs are usually covered with stuff and that makes it hard for her to get to her bedroom. I told her that after that, she should move on to one of the rooms. Then, section by section, her home would get cleaned. And she did this. When she finished cleaning her stairs, she started with another area and then moved on to another. In the process, she got rid of a lot of things she finally realized she did not need. While her house is not completely cleaned up, she's now happy tidying it up. Many other things in our lives are like that. We can work our way out of difficulties if we do it incrementally. The most important ingredient of transformation is to concretely establish self-confidence.

Chan teachings are practical. They do not focus on lofty, abstract theories. "Look at what's under your feet" is a famous Chan saying. Someone once asked Chan master Yunmen (864–949), "What's buddhahood?" he replied, "Who's asking?!" Another person asked him how to be free and

Yunmen said, "Who is binding you?" Right here, right now, we are the ones who can answer this question. Just take care of this moment, one step at a time. If you start thinking of the future—"When will I ever become awakened?"—then you will miss what is right under your feet! If you are always looking ahead, worrying about how to climb to the top of the mountain, then you will never get there. You will give up even attempting the climb, thinking it's too arduous or long, and you'll end up feeling discouraged. Focus instead on the present; on what's under your feet as you take each step, and before you know it, you will find yourself on top of the mountain.

Ruminating about the past and projecting onto the future obstructs our present. Worse, it leads to mistakes. Those who do mountain climbing know this. It is the same with practice. I'm not saying we should never plan for the future; of course, we should, but once we've set a task for ourselves, we should follow through step by step. This will strengthen our self-confidence, which will lead us to our destination. Yet we should also have flexibility. When causes and conditions change, we may have to adapt to them, but our general direction doesn't have to change.

Sometimes people don't lack confidence in themselves, but they doubt the teachings. There are many teachings that are beyond our understanding. The way to work with this is to engage with what we can and keep an open mind about what we currently don't understand. As our practice deepens, we will come to appreciate the deeper significance of those teachings.

Confidence is also connected to wisdom. The *Mahaprajnaparamita-shastra* states, "Faith allows us to enter the ocean of buddhadharma, but it is wisdom that delivers."[1] The significance of this passage points to the interconnection between faith and wisdom. To have confidence or faith in something is to have an attitude of openness. It is precisely this openness that allows us to transcend our self-referential attachments. Our personal experience mediates between our faith and wisdom. When we encounter a teaching, we don't just believe in it; we have to personally experience it. In this way, faith *becomes* wisdom. This is why "faith enters, and wisdom delivers."

DETERMINATION

Confidence and continuous effort together give rise to the prerequisite of determination. Usually when we think of determination, we think of diligent practice like a tidal wave. We give it our all, and, in the process, we become tense. But this kind of determination is usually contaminated by greed and anger, which are unwholesome mental factors. "I want to realize awakening; I want to attain buddhahood. I want this, I want that."

Once a student asked Master Linji (d. 866) how to escape samsara, the sea of birth and death. Linji said, "That's samsara!" I'm sure the questioner was earnest and determined, but that very desire to escape is grasping! If you are already practicing the dharma, there is no need for you to always ruminate about liberation. Just practice, and when the seeking mind ceases, awakening is realized.

Most of the time, we are driven by our need to grasp or reject. This is not determination. Determination may be directed—as when we make vows—but it is not directed by greed. Don't think about your own gain, and never give up helping others. Engage in practice with contentment, interest, confidence, and determination. Don't let your practice be fueled by grasping, rejecting, disinterest, or self-disparagement.

Determination is about being steadfast, trickling on like a fine stream in a continuous flow that does not end. Even when a big boulder is in the way, the stream simply meanders around it and continues. So a Chan analogy for determination is a continuous stream of water, without gaps, without seams. This attitude helps us to keep the body and mind relaxed, without grasping, and at the same time, diligent. This takes discipline and resourcefulness.

Normally, when people are tired, they are unable to practice. But when they are clear, they practice very well. But we have to be able to practice in all situations, even when we're tired. Being resourceful is learning to adapt to the conditions of our bodies and minds; that's how we become skillful practitioners. So how do we practice when we're fatigued? If we try to fight through the fatigue, we will become more exhausted, and our minds will become more scattered. We have to know when to take a rest. When the mind is agitated or excited, how do we practice? We may need to relax more and bring the energy of the body downward to get grounded. We learn to approach our practice from different angles, adjusting our attitude accordingly. All of this is part of building a relationship with ourselves. When we are skillful, then our practice comes alive. Slowly, it becomes less influenced by the limits of our bodies and minds. This comes with patience and as a result of cultivating all the previous right attitudes.

Sometimes we have to take a step backward in order to go forward. In practice, going backward is not necessarily regression. Advancing forward is not necessarily progression. We have to assess our practice honestly. For example, on retreat, sometimes if we push ourselves too much, allowing our grasping mind to seep in, we then become scattered, and thoughts just come flooding in. In those occasions, we have to let the body and mind rest and give ourselves a break.

In whatever situation you find yourself, never say "I can't." Instead, ask yourself, "How will I practice?" If you say, "I can't," the gate of Chan is closed. If you ask, "How?" then a pathway opens. Don't be limited by our narratives about what we can or can't do. In reality, there's nothing that can't be accomplished if we put our minds to it.

These attitudes—contentment, interest, confidence, and determination—complement one another. We must cultivate them together. Sometimes we need one more than the others; other times, we need to develop them together. Or, we may explore them one at a time, but the others are always in the background. Practice is an organic process, and each of us is different, so we have to be in tune with the undercurrents of our own interior states and know how to respond. When in doubt, ask the teacher for guidance.

5. Meditation

THE ATTITUDES detailed above are forms of meditation in and of themselves because they involve self-cultivation. With the right cultivation, our meditation includes all aspects of life: the way we relate to ourselves and others, the way we carry ourselves in daily life, the way we engage with various tasks, the way we live and die. However, we have to start simply before we can really cultivate practice in the complexity of daily life. We do this by practicing seated meditation and simple physical actions like walking and cleaning, where we are not distracted by too many engagements; where we can face our habits and learn to adjust our attitude accordingly. Whenever we meditate, we actually bring to our practice our baggage of emotional afflictions and habits. It is precisely because of this that we need to expose, embrace, work through, and let go of these afflictions. This is how we align ourselves with our true nature.

We are so used to being caught up in our thoughts and feelings that we lose sight of our true nature. The key to meditation is to recognize that the host is not the guest. The comings and goings of thoughts and feelings are like guests coming into our homes. Would you let guests run your house? Of course not. You're the host. You may consult them, but you must be the one to make any final decisions. Most of the time, trouble comes when we listen to the guests—our fleeting thoughts and feelings—and ignore our responsibility as hosts. For example, some people are extremely affected by self-disparaging thoughts. But why should our happiness depend on passing thoughts? Our true nature, buddha-nature, is already free and liberated.

Who *is* the host, though? That's the million-dollar question. How do we recognize our true nature? We have to use a method of practice with the right attitudes of contentment and great interest. These two primary attitudes reveal the Chan principles of no-thought, no-form, and non-abiding, as well as the prerequisites of confidence and determination. With these right attitudes, we will be able to directly perceive the host.

Our practice will flourish when we have the right attitudes. Depending on whether we're scattered or drowsy, energetic or fatigued, clear or hazy, a method of practice can be used in a relaxed or intensive way. A method is not fixed. We make it come alive with the attitude we bring to it. Most of us have to start with a relaxed approach. Why? Because most of us are very tense, whether we realize it or not. With a tense body and mind, it is impossible to see what kind of attitude we're bringing to our practice. And while a more intense practice can be an antidote for a lazy or hazy practice, it cannot last long. The ability to practice with intensity takes skillfulness, because the body should be completely relaxed with only the mind focused wakefully on the method. Thus, the intense approach is established on the foundation of relaxation. The first thing to learn, then, is a relaxed method of practice.

Priming the Body and Mind

First, it is best to prepare yourself for seated meditation by doing mindful stretches to help the body become limber so its energy can flow more smoothly. The mind also becomes collected and centered, in tune with the body. Preparing the body and mind in this way builds a transition from activity to stillness. Then, you can effectively engage with your sitting practice.

The mindful self-massage and yoga stretches I teach target particular areas of the body that tend to get very tense (a description of these stretches and accompanying photographs appear on the Tallahassee Chan Center website, tallahasseechan.org). Many people come to meditation with stiff bodies or even old injuries, so while their muscles and bones may be healed, energy blocks may still be present. Blocks may also come from repetitive actions like typing on a computer, which can cause shoulder pain. Stretching mindfully can help alleviate this and other kinds of pain.

The energy blockages from postural stress relate to *qi* (pronounced *chee*). In traditional Chinese thought, qi is that which constitutes the body, mind, and world—it is the building block of everything. Qi travels throughout the body, but tension and injuries can cause qi blockage.

Many of us are habituated to tensing up throughout the day. Due to our postures while sitting or working, we may have pain in different areas of our bodies. For some of us, even certain words or images can trigger tension.

Every time these scenarios arise, the body responds in a certain way. These are signs that our bodies have learned to respond to situations with tension, and there's a qi blockage. So we start our practice by taking care of the body. By doing yoga stretches to make the body limber and relaxed, we are breaking the patterns of conditioning.

SEATED MEDITATION

Before you sit, remove your glasses or any tight objects on your body like watches, bracelets, or belts. Choose a stable posture that you can maintain for thirty minutes without much discomfort. You'd be surprised how long you can sit with the right attitude, preparation, and method. Generally, a good posture is one that allows your back to be naturally upright, with each vertebra stacked on top of the other. This usually means using the support of a cushion so that your buttocks are higher than your knees. Thus supported, your lower back will regain its natural curve and your spine will be straight. Your ears should be in alignment with your shoulders so that the weight of your head doesn't pull it forward, and it can be sustained effortlessly by the neck. Move your head around, back and forth and side to side, until you find the perfect point of balance. When you do, your vertebrae, neck, and head will align perfectly at the center. Once you're seated properly, then you can prime the body for sitting by deliberately relaxing.

Begin a progressive relaxation from head to toe, by placing your awareness on each body part and feeling its accompanying sensations. Don't think, but experience the sensations of the body. To practice progressive relaxation, first feel your whole body. Then bring your awareness to the crown of your head. Feel the sensations there and extend your awareness to your scalp. Allow even each follicle of your hair to relax. Now, slowly allow your awareness to flow down to your forehead. Feel the space between your eyebrows. Relax. Raise your eyebrows slowly and then let them drop. Tense and relax; tense and relax. Do this a few times so you become familiar with what it feels like to relax this area of your face.

Now move to your eyes. Don't use your eyes to see anything—it doesn't matter if they are open or closed. If you see darkness, that means you are using your eyes. Treat your eyeballs like muscles. Feel their contours and weight, and then relax them. We hold a lot of tension in the eyes, and because of this, our attention is in the head. We are not grounded but live in our thoughts instead. So let your eyes, eyebrows, forehead, and scalp relax.

Next, relax your cheeks and lips. Tuck in your chin. Soften and moisten your lips, and let a gentle smile appear at the corners of your mouth. This will help to relax your facial muscles. Take a moment to feel the subtle shift of the undercurrent feeling tone. Enjoy the smile. Do this to prime your body and mind for sitting.

Feel the sensations down your neck, perhaps at the spot where your clothes touch the skin, then down to your shoulders. The shoulders are also difficult to relax. Lift them up toward your ears and then let them drop. Do this a few times. Focus on the tactile sensation of your shoulders relaxing.

Move down your arms, your biceps, your triceps, and elbows, then your forearms and wrists. Feel the warmth of your palms resting on your knees or in your lap. Relax your fingertips. Relax the skin, muscles, and tendons by feeling them. Move your fingertips if you'd like to bring your awareness to the sensations there. Check your shoulders and arms again—are they relaxed?

Place your attention on the chest. No need to push it out, just be natural. Feel the subtle rise and fall of your chest following the rhythm of your breath. Relax. Feel the center of gravity there, and allow that gravity to drop down further as you exhale, moving down to your abdomen. Feel the subtle rise and fall of your abdomen as it also follows the rhythm of your breath. Relax.

In meditation, your abdomen must be relaxed. The abdomen is yet another area in which we hold tension. If you don't know how to relax here, then place your palm over your abdomen and feel the slight movement of your stomach rising and falling, rising and falling with the rhythm of your breath. If you can feel this, then your abdomen is relaxed. If not, your posture may be causing your abdomen to tense up. Check if you are sitting high enough on your cushion so that the lumbar area is naturally curved.

Now that the front part of the body is basically relaxed, focus on the back. From the back of the neck, relax down the shoulder blades. Use your exhalations to help you relax: As you exhale, release any tension in the upper back, then with the next exhalation relax down the middle of your back. Exhale, and relax the lower back.

Now feel your whole body weight on the buttocks. Feel your center of gravity rooted to the seat, to earth. Feel the sensation of the cushion under you. You may sway your body from left to right and front to back to see if you are centered. Sometimes we lean to one side or the other when we subtly hold tension. Find your center of gravity and then let your body weight drop. Allow all of the weight of the upper body to settle downward to the earth, to the ground. Feel your upper body to be light as a feather.

The last step is relaxing your hips, thighs, legs, all the way down to your feet and toes. Now place your hands in the meditation posture on your lap: two palms facing up, left hand on top of right, two thumbs touching, forming an oval shape. You may use towels in your lap and place your palms there in order to help support your hands. Try doing this progressive relaxation several times from head to toe until you're relaxed.

There are some scientific studies that show the physical benefits of relaxation. Not that we need to know this—we just have to practice it. But for those who are curious, consciously practicing relaxation engages the circuitry of our parasympathetic nervous system (PNS). Not only does this practice relax our body, it also strengthens the neural pathways of the PNS and may actually reverse cellular damage from chronic stress and prevent further damage from happening.

Developing a practice of progressive relaxation is very important and has many benefits. It strengthens our ability to relax, both in meditation and in daily life. It enhances our brain's flexibility (i.e., neuroplasticity) and encourages us to relax. Neuroscientists find that relaxation stimulates the *nucleus basalis*—a group of neurons that permeates the neocortex—to secrete a neurotransmitter called acetylcholine. Acetylcholine is what enables neurons that are activated at the same time to strengthen their connections to each other. This means the more we cultivate a relaxed body and mind, the stronger our ability to be relaxed under different circumstances is. When we're faced with difficulties, we are able to respond with composure.[1]

After we prime the body for sitting, we need to prime the mind. So take a moment to feel your subtle smile again. Become aware of the pleasant feeling that accompanies it; experience contentment and joy. Savor this feeling for a few moments. See that there's no need to grasp or reject anything. Your heart is content, in the present. Then, having primed the body and mind, take up your method for meditation.

BREATH

An excellent method of meditation is mindfulness of the breath, which serves as a foundation for more advanced methods of practice. Having relaxed and grounded the body, having attuned your attitude to contentment, you will be able to simply be aware of the in and out movement of the breath at the nostrils without distractions. If you don't go through the progressive relaxation and the adjustment of your attitude, then you will not recognize what's going on inside you and how you are bringing all kinds of baggage to your sitting period—for example, tension in the body or a subtle agitation of mind. But having primed the body and mind, your breath will be harmonized, inaudible, refined, subtle, and steady. It should not be audible, coarse, or unsteady. If it is, that means the body is not relaxed, so go back to progressive relaxation. If your breath is subtle, you will notice in it all sorts of sensations from cool to warm, silky to coarse, light to heavy, in addition to just the in and out itself. In fact, as you progress, the notion of in and out will subside, leaving you with just these sensations.

There are all sorts of signposts to progressive stages of mindfulness of breath such as concentration and clarity, and these are natural occurrences during our meditation. But they're not something we need to seek, for they're simply like the changing scenery as you travel down a road. The scenery is not the destination. Don't grasp at it, just keep going. For example, as you continue to count steadily, even the sensation of your breath at the nostrils will fade, leaving you with simply the presence of breath at the tip of your nose. If your mind is clear and focused, without wandering thoughts, and the breath has become so subtle that there seems to be no breath, then at this time bring your awareness to the subtle experience of the rise and fall of your abdomen. Maintain your concentration there. This would be the next signpost or stage of meditation on the breath. Follow the rhythm of your breath through the rise and fall of your abdomen, and just continue with a clear and wakeful mind.

Again, right attitude is most important; it shapes our experience of the method. If your mind is grasping or seeking after something "special," then it will be agitated and unable to develop focus and clarity. Similarly, if you're bored, believing that you already know how to breathe, then you will lose interest and become scattered or fall asleep. If you love someone and are interested in being with this person, would you fall asleep while engaged with them? No. So in practicing mindfulness of the breath, you have to feel content and at ease. As far as you're concerned, the mind can think all it wants; you are happy to be in the present with your breath. At the same time, you're fascinated with the various sensations of the breath in each moment. Every moment is experienced as fresh and new. You're in love with your method. This is the direct application of the correct attitudes of contentment and great interest.

Continuing with the rise and fall of your abdomen, we gradually progress to the next signpost or stage where the abdomen's rise and fall is no longer perceptible and the presence of yourself sitting is most prominent. So just sit wakefully. At this point, you could meditate on the natural expression of silent illumination—mind as *experiencing*.

6. Approaches to Silent Illumination

Silent Illumination as Embodied Experiencing

In reality, there is no fixed "path." But when we use a method of practice, a path is created. Think of a duck crossing the river; the river has no set path but as the duck swims across, it leaves a trail. Then the trail disappears but the duck finds itself on the other side of the river. The trail, the method, comes alive when we use it. Likewise, there is no fixed method of silent illumination. We use a method in our practice and it reveals our hindrances. Through this process, we work through and let go of them. When we practice in this way, then silent illumination, or our awakened nature, manifests.

One main method for silent illumination is what I call embodied experiencing. It's an antidote to the fact that most people live in their heads. They are top-heavy, so whatever method they use, they tend to turn it into thinking. Embodied experiencing, particularly in sitting meditation practice, counters this as we experience the presence of the body moment to moment. Experiencing the body is not about thinking. Instead, it is being *in* the body, *with* the body, and *experiencing* it concretely. It is an embodied experience.

In sitting, we learn how to rest in the body yet wakefully experience our sitting. Basically, this method is simple: Experience being in the body sitting relaxed and awake. This may sound easy, but it is the key. We need to learn it. It is the most natural, uncontrived way to practice, and it avoids the problem of living in our heads.

The mind has no stages, no levels, no front and back, up and down. The different stages of practice that we experience are only general signposts along the trajectory of scattered mind, concentrated mind, unified mind, and no-mind or no self-referential mind, which is the state of awakening. Yet this formulation is a prescription, a map. A map is not the territory. The description and the reality of how things actually work are quite different.

Not everyone will experience these stages. Some people practicing at the first stage might suddenly enter into Chan and see their self-nature.

Some practitioners hold on to these stages, "imagining" themselves going through them. But we don't need to work our way through the first, second, third, and fourth stages until eventually we're enlightened. They are merely expedient means. All we need to do is practice in this moment. Forget about the future or past, environment and body. Just be in the present, *experiencing* your sitting wholeheartedly and never belittling who you are. In moment-to-moment experiencing, body and mind are one; stillness and wakefulness are one; concentration and clarity are one.

Our experiencing in this very moment is the expression of the workings of our true nature, buddha-nature. What we need to drop away are emotional afflictions, the veil that conceals our true nature. Thus, the single most important principle for seated meditation is *experiencing*.

When my teacher, Master Sheng Yen, was in his late forties and early fifties, he taught silent illumination without stages. But in the latter part of his life, he taught it as a gradual path with stages of practice. He taught it this way out of kindness for people so they could hold on to something concrete. Even though he had clearly stated that the stages are expedient means or signposts, students typically ignored that teaching and strove to practice silent illumination as if there were real stages on the path. I, too, have written on silent illumination in terms of the various stages of practice.[1] But I no longer teach it this way because people inevitably start to attach to the signposts.

In teaching the practice of experiencing, I discovered that many people start to imagine themselves sitting. Somehow they place themselves outside of themselves and watch themselves sitting. This is completely wrong! Body and mind are already together in sitting. We simply need to embody the experiencing. How? Simply *experiencing* sitting! In doing this, no words or labels are needed. All opposites are dissolved. Don't get caught up with that which is experienced—the body, sitting, and the one experiencing sitting. Let there just be moment-to-moment *experiencing*. As long as there is experiencing in this moment, there is already quiescent wakefulness.

Experiencing is itself fresh and open, relaxed and wakeful. In it, there is no division between body and mind. But to begin, you need an anchor. So feel the presence of the body grounded on the earth; that is, clearly feel the presence of the body sitting. When your body sits, your mind sits. Body is sitting, mind is sitting. There is no separation. But if you are self-conscious—if you are looking at your body from outside of yourself—you are not experiencing sitting. You are creating an experiencer and that which is experienced. Never visualize the body sitting or *think* about the body sitting. Simply be in the body, in its presence, and stay grounded there.

In just sitting, body and mind are just this act of sitting, this reality. Sitting is not a concept—there are no conceptual descriptions or labels that define it. It is completely embodied. Don't get caught up with the particulars of the body-mind experience, either. Just concretely experience *being here*, sitting.

If you don't need an object or an anchor, then experience the experiencing itself. In the stream of being in the present, moment to moment, there's simply *being* and *experiencing*. The present moment and experiencing are not two separate things. There are no objects of the mind, and there is no subject needed to meditate on this or that object. Self is not needed. The experiencing itself is the present moment. The present moment is already free.

A common problem with practitioners is mistaking self-consciousness with clarity or mindfulness. Self-consciousness belongs to the level of discursive thinking. It is a little voice, a judgment about being aware of yourself, objectifying yourself as a *thing*: "Hey, I'm doing it! I'm doing silent illumination!" or "Am I doing this right?" or "Should I practice like this?" All of these are just wandering thoughts. At the center of them, there's a strong sense of me, I, and mine.

But being unified in body and mind, clear and wakeful, is not awakening either. This is not true silent illumination, but at least it is a natural state of being, aligned with our self-nature. Why? Because in this moment, there is still the subtle clear rising and ceasing of "me sitting." Even though the self is not so prominent, even though we are simply being present with our experiencing, this clarity is the fundamental mind of birth and death. It is not awakening.

Master Yongjia Xuanjue articulated this state as, "If you are aware of this awareness of stillness, then this is not the unconditioned awareness."[2] This "being aware of this awareness of stillness" is fundamental ignorance—the self. Even though the crude forms of craving, aversion, arrogance, and so on have subsided, subtle forms of self-attachment still exist.

An analogy for this state is a nicely cleaned window. Although the window is clearly transparent, there's still a window there after all. Practice is like cleaning the window. It is not like writing or scribbling on bits of paper, writing stories about what we are seeing, making up theories about what's inside and outside. There's an expression for this, isn't there? "We are the authors of our own lives." Practice is different. It's more like noticing that the window is not very clean, that it might be obscuring what's out there, so we start to clean it. The more we focus on the window, the more we realize that it really is quite dirty. All the conditioning, all the years of marking up the window with our notions, beliefs, habit tendencies—all these markings are stuck to the glass and make it hard to see. So we start to clean. We scrape and polish and clean until the window is quite clear. We recognize all our conditioning, and we let it drop away.

Then the window becomes very clear—so clear that it's almost as if it's not there. It's so clean that a person might try to walk through it or a bird might fly into it, but there is still a window there. There is still a divide between us and what is on the other side. This clear window is a close approximation to experiencing without contrivance, to wakefulness without wandering thoughts. But it is not the true clarity of awakening. The window, however clear it may be, is still there. The self, however absent it may appear to be, is still present. And even though it might seem that there is no window, because it is so clear, we eventually realize that there is still a "window" there. How? We encounter some obstacle and the window becomes an obstruction. For example, a bird bangs against the window. Or we lean forward and hit our forehead and experience pain. As long as the self is present, we will experience obstructions and suffering.

The self *is* attachment. When there is attachment, there are obstructions. What is attachment? It is whatever we can't let go of. Some people think that a clear window is true clarity. They call it "naked awareness," or "choiceless awareness," or "selfless awareness" because it is so clear, seemingly without self. But that clarity becomes a source of attachment.

The difference between this clear window and no window at all is like night and day. The clarity of seeing through a clear window that is well polished and free of marks or streaks is nice, but it is very different from having no window at all! When the self is absent, there is no window at all and no obstructions anywhere. Originally, there is no window.

This process has infinite possibilities because there are infinite obstructions, infinite modes of conditioning. As we proceed, we may experience different altered states but they are still just marks on the window. In practice, we keep on polishing until we have a clear window. And then we let go of the window. We realize there never was a need for a window in the first place. We don't need self-reference in order to live, to love, and to be successful and productive. In fact, it is the self that limits our potential. Self-reference or self-attachment is a fabrication. We've mistaken our brain's sense of subjectivity as the presence of a permanent self. It is true that we need this sense of self to navigate the world—when we see a red light we need to stop and when we feel pain we need to heal because, in a conventional sense, the world is there and we are in it. But there is absolutely no need to reify, solidify, and attach to something that is inherently changing and non-abiding. There is no fixed self-image, self-concern, and self-reference. We are free!

Sitting in this wakeful clarity, there's just this moment-to-moment experiencing. Most of the time, a person's wakeful clarity is dependent upon objects and the apprehension of objects. It is dependent on a kind of self-referential, conditioned consciousness. When the conditions are there, illumination is present; when the conditions subside, the mind is not clear anymore. The conditions include a whole host of things like the condition of our bodies, our level of energy, the rhythm of our habits throughout the day, the presence or lack of a supportive environment for practice, and so on. So in this practice we have to be clear about what is actually happening in the moment without employing our usual self-referential habits. Whatever arises, we just experience everything effortlessly. Again, this is contentment but with great interest.

By just experiencing, we save energy. We don't make anything into a *thing*. The body is not an "object" and we don't make it into a thing on which we meditate. Mind is not a thing either. Making something into a thing is attachment. Attachments take energy; they waste energy. The principle of silent illumination is not about creating or fabricating something. If we have to fabricate something, then it would be something we have to continue to create and maintain. This is an impossible task! Self-nature is not something we create moment to moment and hold onto. This is the wrong way to practice.

Experiencing is just what we do. It is the most natural way of being. We don't have to create or fabricate anything because, moment to moment, we are already experiencing. This experiencing is the most natural, effortless state. If we practice like this, without fabricating anything, we begin to align ourselves more and more with our true nature, with how things actually are.

Some people practice just sitting by watching the body like a corpse. Don't do that. Just experience. There's no need to create a concept or label anything as a "body." When we sit, we don't reify, solidify, or congeal either the body or the present moment into a thing. We would tie ourselves up into knots if we did that. Every moment is a new beginning; every moment is already fresh—moment-to-moment experiencing. This experiencing is palpable, not abstract. If we create a body and then observe it, then we are meditating on an abstract idea or concept. As a result, we will develop a headache or some other side effect. On the other hand, practicing silent illumination through embodied experiencing—this is truly the method of ease and bliss.

SILENT ILLUMINATION AS DIRECT CONTEMPLATION

What I have outlined above is a way to practice silent illumination through an embodied experiencing of sitting. Once we are adept at doing this, we will no longer need the body as a support. We can simply maintain the clarity of *experiencing*. But there are other approaches to silent illumination, and one of them is called "direct contemplation."

Direct contemplation is sensory training. It is a way of perceiving things in their clarity, free from distortion, fabrication, and conceptualization. "Direct" means the nonconceptual awareness that is free from words and notions. "Contemplation" here means experiencing. It does not mean reflecting or thinking in any way. The key is no conceptualization, no labeling or naming or forming ideas about the object that we are perceiving. These are just constructs that we project onto the objects of perception. They are not a true reflection of reality.

To engage in direct contemplation, we meditate on sight or sound without distorting it through our concepts. To be undistorted, our perception must be totally free from conceptual elaborations. Of course, other things can cause distortion. We may have a defect in our eye or ear, or the object of contemplation may be moving quickly so that it causes an optical illusion, like a spinning light that seems to form a ring of fire. Or perhaps the external situation makes it difficult to practice direct contemplation—for example, if we're on a moving train and looking out the window. However, the most common hindrance to direct contemplation is our own mental state—the subtle underlying feeling tones that are affecting our present contemplation and giving rise to conceptual elaboration.

Again, we must not engage with words, labels, comparisons, discriminations, and concepts of any kind. This is the meaning of "direct." We just experience sight and sound in all of their clarity in the present moment. We don't elaborate on what we see or hear and we don't lose focus either. *Experiencing* is a cornerstone of direct contemplation as it is understood within the Buddhist theory of perception.

The method of direct contemplation is similar to what modern philosophers call a "perceptual reduction."[3] We empty our minds without closing them completely to the external world. In this state of liminal awareness, a state without forming or projecting concepts and ideas onto things, everything appears to us but we do not identify objects. We merely let them be. When we come out of this state, the usual conceptual flow returns and with it the ability to identify things.

Owing to the speed of the mental process, we usually cannot differentiate conceptual from nonconceptual perception. Only in some situations, like the meditative state of direct contemplation, can a clear differentiation be made. There, the flow of wandering thought gradually subsides, and we reach a state in which we simply experience sight or sound. For example, in directly contemplating sight, shapes and colors are seen but we don't label them—there are no conceptual interpretations.

I normally teach this method by employing visual or auditory perception as the support for practice. These two perceptions are vivid because they are produced by the presence of clear objects—sight and sound. Usually we only have a vague idea of perception, and it is hard for us to separate perceptions from language and concepts. Most of our experiences are usually mediated by concepts. We are completely engrossed with words and language, and we can't tell the difference between what we think about an object and the object itself. Direct contemplation is a very useful method for freeing ourselves from the overlay of words and labels that we impose on the world. It allows us to just experience things as they are.

Before I discuss how to use this method of direct contemplation in detail, however, I need to introduce the nature of perception in relation to practice. You may find the following section a bit theoretical, but stay with it—it will help you understand what's going on in your practice. When you clearly understand how perception works, you will be able to better appreciate and apply the method of direct contemplation. This section should also clear up some of the misconceptions about awareness, or "mindfulness" in popular Buddhism, along with New Age terms such as "naked awareness." After the theory, I will discuss how it is relevant in actual practice.

There are four types of "bare perception" as detailed in the Yogachara or "consciousness-only" tradition of Buddhism. These are sensory, mental, self-cognizant, and yogic.[4] "Bare" means it is nondeceptive and direct, without conceptualization. Only the fourth type—yogic—is considered to be a state of experiential awakening.

The first, direct sensory perception, refers to the initial moment of our experience of sight, sound, smell, taste, and touch. One early school of Buddhism, the Vaibhashika or "realist" school, taught that consciousness actually apprehends "external" objects directly with no intermediary processes. This is partially why adherents of this school are called realists: they believe there are real *things* out there. However, later Mahayana Yogachara masters taught that consciousness apprehends external objects indirectly, through the mediation of what is called "aspects." In Yogachara, these aspects are the marks, signs, and imprints of the object in consciousness. So what we're experiencing are imprints of the sense objects—not the objects themselves.

This theory is analogous to modern neuroscientists' notion that what we experience as sight, for example, is actually a "simulation" by the visual cortex of the brain. When light from an external object impinges on our visual receptors, only 10 percent of the information contained in the visual stimulus—of what we think we are seeing—is needed in order for the brain to construct an internal image or representation of it. The other 90 percent of that image is the result of simulations produced by the brain's own activity. That is, 90 percent of the object we "see" is made up! It is simply a collection of electrochemical signals which then interact with our internal memories and cognition (which also consists of electrochemical signals). In other words, we have never actually lived in the world "out there." We've been living in a simulated world. Now, it's not to say that the world doesn't exist; it's just that we've never lived in it.

This is similar to what Yogachara teachers mean when they talk about the "aspects" of an object acting as mediators of our experience. As radical as this may sound, essentially *all* objects are constructs of the mind. This is a crucial point because it explains the relationship between consciousness and the external world. So bare visual perception is not the experience of "bare seeing" at all, but rather the experience of an "aspect" of sight. This "aspect" is a property of consciousness, not of the external object.

In the direct contemplation of a tree or a prairie, for example, what we're contemplating or experiencing is an aspect or imprint of each of these before the label "tree" or "prairie" comes into being. Yogachara Buddhism recognizes a stage *before* the visual cortex simulates an object—whether it is a tree or a prairie. It is an instantaneous quickening of perception that is not yet a full-fledged representation or concept. In neuroscience, the simulated construct of the visual field is actually a full-fledged conceptual representation.

In the Buddhist teaching of what constitutes a human being—the five aggregates or skandhas (i.e., form, sensation, conception, volition, and consciousness)—an "aspect" is actually one of the finer dimensions of sensation. When this sensation is processed by our higher-order brain structures and is conceptualized, then the aspect becomes a conception. Only when it is interpreted by concepts does the aspect become a full-fledged object. Then, in the scheme of the five skandhas, volition happens when we act on the basis of our conception.

The second type of perception is direct mental perception. In Yogachara, consciousness is divided into eight layers. The first five are traditionally referred to as "consciousness" (I like to think of them as cognitive moments) that arise on the basis of our eyes, ears, nose, tongue, and body. The sixth is mental consciousness that arises in the faculty of mind/brain and represents our ability to symbolize, conceive things, discriminate, and so on. The seventh is the self-grasping consciousness that mediates or filters all of our experiences from the previous six layers of consciousness. The eighth is "storehouse" consciousness—the repository of all mental imprints and karmic seeds based on actions of body, speech, and mind. Direct sensory perception correlates to the first five sensory categories of these eight layers of consciousness. Bare mental perception arises almost simultaneously with sensory perception, and both arise immediately prior to conceptualization of the object of perception.[5]

According to Buddhism, true and sustained bare mental perception is the awareness of another person's state of mind—clairvoyance or mind reading. This perception is only available to those who have attained deeper states of meditative absorption, or mental quiescence (Pali *jhana*; Skt. *dhyana*). For most of us, the only true bare mental perceptions that take place are those that occur for extremely brief moments immediately after true sense perceptions, just immediately before conceptualization.[6]

For example, when we remember, imagine, or dream about a sight, sound, smell, taste, or touch, the object of our cognition is an idea or mental representation of the corresponding sense object. This mental representation is already a concept; it is a full-fledged construct we are generating with our minds. However, a bare mental perception is a nonconceptual mental aspect created through the apparatus of our mind/brain. This means that when an image appears in our mind, for an instant we have a valid bare mental perception of that image. Then we quickly conceptualize it, which makes our perception invalid. According to the Chinese Yogachara tradition, this direct mental perception should be nonconceptual and without constructed elaborations.

The third type of perception is direct self-cognizant perception. This is similar to what Western philosophers call "apperception," namely, the knowledge that we have of our own mental states. However, it is different from apperception in that self-cognizant perception is not knowledge— it is an intuitive and reflexive experiencing of our inner mental states.[7] Its function is to know our own mental activities, such as craving or aversion.

The above three types of perception may be valid, bare, or direct, but for most, each of these is followed by subsequent cognition and inattentive cognitions.[8] All moments of consciousness go through these three stages. The first moment is always a pristine, bare perception, without conceptualization—it's fresh and direct, such as nonconceptual experiencing of a tree or prairie. The second is called subsequent perception, which is a continuing reproduction of the same apprehension of a tree or prairie. It is no longer fresh (unless we engage in direct contemplation) because we're conceptually fabricating the tree or prairie. Then the last moment is inattentive perception: that is, our attention drifts away from the tree or prairie to something else. Inattentive cognition happens when we engage in direct contemplation of a tree or prairie but we also notice birds flying by and other things.

The fourth and final type of direct perception is yogic perception, which is never inattentive. This is the mind-stream of a person who's either in the state of awakening or is thoroughly awakened.[9] What I mean here is that a person may have had an experience of awakening, but may not always be in that state—self-grasping may return. A thoroughly awakened person is always in the state of awakening. Bare yogic perception arises from prajna, or selfless wisdom, and with it, we experience things in two ways. First, we apprehend the ultimate truth of a thing: emptiness. Second, we apprehend the conventional truth of a thing: wondrous existence, or the workings of causes and conditions. In the former, we perceive the impermanence of the five skandhas, the emptiness of self, and so on, and in the latter case, we perceive the various useful and seemingly permanent qualities of the sense of me, I, and mine. We can also navigate through life learning to recognize, adapt, wait for, and create various conditions. We simultaneously understand what we are and how we exist.

For people who have had genuine awakening, even if they are not *in* the state of awakening, they are most likely able to sustain some degree of attentive perception in daily life. I say "most likely" because some people's experience of no-self is so shallow and short-lived that it has no real effect on their lives; it's more like a temporary absence of self-grasping. Without diligent cultivation, such an experience remains a mere memory. It is like not having the experience at all. It's definitely possible for these people to be inattentive in daily life. They can even break precepts and harm others. Why? Because when self-grasping is present, craving, aversion, and ignorance are also still present.

This brief survey presents a Buddhist epistemological basis for the teaching of direct contemplation. Direct contemplation is contemplation based on bare sensory perception—the first of the four types of perception recognized in Yogachara Buddhism. When we actually practice this method, however, we don't think about any of these things. We simply engage with sight or sound directly, refraining from conceptualizing what we see or hear.

My teacher used direct contemplation as a supporting method primarily because our eyes and ears cannot sustain us in meditation for long periods of time; we tend to get tired. Thus, the effectiveness of this method is limited. However, in my experience, it is still possible to integrate direct contemplation into one's formal method by contemplating sight or sound. It is just that at a certain point, we must shift the object of contemplation slightly.

For example, after contemplating the bare perception of sound for a while, we can shift the contemplation to the simple *experiencing* itself. The object of sound drops away. This directly segues into the embodied experiencing of sitting that I teach above. After a while, the body drops away and we are just simply *experiencing* moment to moment until subject and object both cease to be. But we must let go of even this state to realize awakening, which is the fulfillment of silent illumination.

In Yogachara terms, if we're able to engage in direct contemplation of sound, practice steadily, and refrain from formulating concepts, then it is possible for us to experience bare mental perception after sound drops away—in other words, the second of the four types of direct perception (see above). If we continue, there is simply the experiencing, which is the third type of bare perception: self-cognizant perception, where we are simply aware of the experiencing without external support, without conceptualization. Our perception remains a direct perceptual experience. When this experiencing drops away, self-reference drops away too. This is the fourth type of bare yogic perception.

The actual practice of direct contemplation through sound, for example, is pretty straightforward, and I usually lead this practice outdoors in a natural setting. The method is this: First, sit stably as you normally would. Go through the method of progressive relaxation. Second, once you're grounded and relaxed, choose an object that is steady and clear—say the sound of a flowing stream, the constant humming sound in cities, the steady sound of an air-conditioning vent. If you choose a sound that is constantly changing, like birds chirping, classical music, and so on, then it may be more difficult to go deeply into the method because when the various sounds stop, your method is gone too! So stay with a relatively constant sound. Third, refrain from using words, labels, or concepts to identify the sound—let it be what it is with an open heart. Let the sound come to you. Don't focus on the sound intensely. This method is more of an open awareness method, as opposed to single-minded concentration. Fourth, in time, the sound itself will drop away, leaving you with just experiencing. This is the bare mental perception of experiencing as spoken of above.

In the beginning, you may not be able to help yourself from labeling whatever you're hearing. That's fine. Just keep experiencing the sound as it is. Let go of your labeling, and return to the sound. Don't judge. As I stated above, the sound that you are experiencing is really an aspect or imprint of the sound. The point is to learn to hear sounds as they are, without distorting them with labels, concepts, and discriminations. Maintain the freshness of experiencing sound.

Bring the right attitudes of contentment and great interest to your contemplation. Be wakeful, open, and receptive. This wakefulness keeps you on the sound. The open, not-knowing attitude allows you to not engage in labeling what you're hearing. Even if you're only able to do this for a short while, it is already very good, because usually we project all sorts of concepts, narratives, or ideas onto what we're hearing.

In the *Shurangama-sutra*, which describes the contemplation-of-sound method used by Avalokiteshvara, the bodhisattva of compassion, it says this is the state when "the stream of sound, and the subject that perceives [the sound], become quiescent."[10] Basically this happens when we and sound are inseparable. At that point, sound does not exist for us, but we still continue to experience hearing.

If we continue, the experiencing of bare mental perception continues.

Is there sound? No. Is there hearing? Yes. In this state, we maintain a continuity of energy. When this energy is maintained with no interruption, it can be said it is a kind of hearing. In this state, there is no perception of movement or stillness, sound or silence. We are in a meditative absorption. If we do not grasp or abide in this state, eventually we will experience no-self or awakening.

Practice is not linear, but we basically begin with, first, directly contemplating sounds; then, second, the sound ceases, leaving only the experiencing of silence. At this point the sensory perception of sound shifts to experiencing the bare mental perception of sound. Third, there is just the ability of hearing. This is the unification of mind where object and subject merge. At this point our hearing ceases; in time, all oppositions cease, and we enter a meditative absorption. But because the subtle self is still there, we must continue. Fourth, only when we completely eradicate duality will awakening occur. However, this is still not complete awakening. Thus, fifth, when even the awakening experience is let go of, this is complete penetration of awakening. At this point there is nothing to contemplate and no one to contemplate sound, yet sound continues. This is the entry into silent illumination through direct contemplation of sound. The same holds true for other sensory experiences, such as sight.

SILENT ILLUMINATION AS CONTEMPLATING SPACE

In the introduction I used the analogy of a spacious room and its furniture as a metaphor for the relationship between our self-nature and thoughts. In meditation practice, contemplation of space is a subset of direct contemplation, using space as a visual support. This is the third approach to silent illumination. The practice is to settle the mind naturally by observing space with an attitude of openness and non-grasping.

In this contemplation, directly gaze into space straight in front with open eyes. Space is unconditioned—not dependent on causes and conditions, similar to the unconditioned nature of mind. Thus, meditating on space is an expedient means for understanding the nature of mind. The key is to gaze into space, then revert the gaze into an embodied experiencing itself. This contemplation is not about having a blank mind, as if we were in a stupor. The mind is alert and clear, without any object or thought. It is in this state that the mind can revert into experiencing itself.

First, do not allow any mental wandering or thoughts of expectation to enter the mind. Do not think of what qualities this state has. Gaze into space like a cat watching over a mouse hole with wakefulness—then relax into the gazing. Relax your eyes. Space is not an object, a *thing*. So don't fix your mind on the wall or whatever is in front of you—don't stare at objects. Space is translucent, clear, without characteristics. As the mind develops concentration, make the shift from gazing into space to relaxing into the visual *experiencing* itself.

When the mind is content, not attracted to anything and without the need to wander, thoughts will not arise. However, if the mind starts to wander, thoughts will arise. If they do, try to recognize them for what they are—insubstantial, just like space. Recognize them as soon as they arise. Gaze at them and then experience space as before. Do not think anything like "I have to stop them" or "I have succeeded in stopping them." Do not feed feelings of satisfaction or disappointment. Thoughts are the results of desire or grasping. When the mind gives rise to grasping, there is also rejecting.

There are many levels of thought, many levels of grasping and rejecting. Some thoughts are coarse, while others are fine. In meditation, fragmented thoughts of the past or the future are considered coarse thoughts; noticing the sound of a passing car—and knowing it is a car and not something else—is a subtler thought. All of these thoughts are results of attraction or repulsion, the results of habitual patterns of grasping and confusion about our self-nature.

Second, whatever kinds of thoughts arise in meditation, know them for what they are. Experience them as the temporary display of the mind, appearing like insubstantial mirages. Allow them to dissolve into the space that you're experiencing.

Third, continuing to meditate like this, you can directly segue into simply experiencing itself without the support of visual space. Again, this is similar to the embodied-experiencing approach to silent illumination. Moment-to-moment experiencing, abiding nowhere, grasping at nothing. Do not get caught up with internal thoughts (no-thought), external appearances (no-form), and do not allow the experiencing to dwell anywhere (non-abiding). Remain content, wakeful, and relaxed.

SILENT ILLUMINATION THROUGH *SHAMATA* AND *VIPASHYANA*

Some teachers define silent illumination as the union of *shamata* and *vipashyana* or calming and insight (Pali, *samata* and *vipassana*). It is not wrong to say that silent illumination is related to the practice of *shamata* and *vipashyana*, but it is wrong to say that they're the same. Silent illumination is awakening; *shamata* and *vipashyana* are just methods.

As a practice, *shamata* and *vipashyana* are typically cultivated either sequentially or in tandem in order to remove obscurations and emotional afflictions. I won't go into detail on the classical methods, though generally, through concentration and calming with the five methods of stilling the mind (i.e., by focusing on impurity, the breath, the qualities of a buddha, the four immeasurables, and causes and conditions),[11] we attain meditative absorption, or *samadhi*. Afterward, we cultivate insight into the nature of mind through the four foundations of mindfulness (i.e., contemplating the body, sensations, mind, and its mental factors) to realize liberative wisdom, or *prajna*. So *shamata* leads to samadhi, and *vipashyana* leads to prajna. In this layout of the path, it is impossible to have insight into our true nature if the mind is scattered. As with a candle, only a steady flame will illuminate the room clearly. If the flame flickers, whatever objects it illuminates will be fuzzy or unclear, or they will appear to move when they are really stationary. So a practitioner would use any of the five methods of stilling the mind to still the mind, then use any of the four foundations of mindfulness to generate insight. These methods are complex and involve many stages. In my opinion, they may be useful for some, but they are convoluted. Practitioners can easily get caught up in stages, insights, and a sense of progress.

In Chan, *shamata* and *vipashyana* or samadhi and prajna are neither separate nor sequential. As the *Platform Scripture* says:

> Samadhi is the essence of prajna. And prajna is the natural function of samadhi. At the time of prajna, samadhi exists. At the time of samadhi, prajna exists. How is it that samadhi and prajna are simultaneous? It is like the light of the lamp. When the lamp exists, there is light. When there is no lamp, there is darkness. The lamp is the essence of light. The light is the natural function of the lamp. Although their names are different, in essence, they are fundamentally identical. The teaching of samadhi and prajna is just like this.[12]

In Chan, the true nature of samadhi is prajna, the selfless wisdom of emptiness. In my analogy of the room, this emptiness is the room's spaciousness. Intrinsically, the room has no furniture or features; it is sign-less. It is just openness itself. Is it spacious because it is without furniture? No. The furniture merely reveals the spaciousness of the room. This is like the *Platform*

Scripture's analogy of the light of a lamp, whose function is to illuminate. From the Chan perspective, calm and wisdom together are the expression of silent illumination—the two aspects of awakening itself.

Another analogy of the simultaneous practice of samadhi and prajna is a reflecting mirror. A mirror doesn't have any fixed image etched onto its surface, yet it reflects all images without adding or subtracting anything. There is nothing to distort. This is the natural function of the awakened mind.

We should not see awakening as a transcendent quality that is far from us. It is right here, right now. Your awareness of reading in this moment is the function of illumination; in this luminous awareness, there are no fixations. Silent illumination is just the natural, lively expression of moment-to-moment experiencing. Technically, we cannot cultivate it—it is simply what we do. Moment-to-moment experiencing! The problem only arises when we reify, solidify that which we experience as a *thing*. In doing so, subject and object are born, and we're stuck.

Understanding this principle, we may use any method in such a way that brings together samadhi and prajna simultaneously. The reason we can practice simultaneously is because samadhi and prajna are the natural essence and function of our minds, even when we are very deluded, even when we have a lot of wandering thoughts. Our minds do not abide anywhere so, by their very nature, our afflictions and suffering liberate themselves moment to moment. We are the ones holding on to them. Through our attachment, they come into existence. There is also a bodily component to our grasping and so, if we have a lot of wandering thoughts, discursive thinking, we just have to relax the body to quiet the angst. Once the body is relaxed, the fuel line for grasping is cut off.

The way to cultivate samadhi and prajna or calming and insight together through the breath method is to allow awareness of breath to be like a reflected image of the mind. Breath does not define our minds; the image is not the mirror. We simply allow the breath to be, without single-mindedly focusing on it. Instant by instant, the quality of breath is different—just as each image reflected in the mirror exists only for an instant. Lively and fresh, interested but not grasping, our attention naturally follows the breath as it comes and goes. Practicing in such a way, we won't enter into single-minded concentration. Instead, our concentration is spacious and open, wakeful and still. We rest peacefully in the nowness of the breath.

This is just one way to apply the simultaneous cultivation of samadhi and prajna to the breath method. You can use the same principle for other methods of practice. The key is approaching the method with the right attitudes of contentment and interest, confidence and determination.

7. Caveats and Pitfalls

Many experiences, both pleasurable and not so pleasurable, arise in meditation. There are many reasons for this. Sometimes it is the way we live that causes these experiences; other times it is our internal psychosomatic conditions that give rise to them. Our attachments and habits also play a big role. It is important to know how to relate to them because a central part of practice is about creating a relationship with ourselves and building a good relationship with the method. Through practice, our lives become easier. We are happier. We realize how fortunate we are to have come to this path.

The way we engage with our method reflects the way we relate to ourselves and others in daily life. We may be the fighting type, and so when we encounter difficulties, we tend to just try to plow through them. Conversely, we may be insecure about ourselves and our abilities, so when we experience difficulties we give up easily, or when we make progress we doubt our accomplishments. Many of us bring to our practice a whole lifetime of hurt and defensiveness, all of the mechanisms we have developed in order to survive. The way we use our method reveals all of our shortcomings and strengths, inadequacies and resourcefulness. Even though we're originally awakened, we have to work through all of these issues.

Below I discuss a few common issues that arise in meditation. There is no one right way to work with them. I encourage you to explore some of these teachings and see which approach works for you.

Tension

Tension is endemic to modern living. Our jobs are often a source of tension. Tension shapes our thoughts, actions, and choices, which in turn create more tension, not only for ourselves but also for those we love. The people closest to us tend to be the ones who get hurt. The first step to making our lives easier—as well as the lives of those around us—is to recognize tension and learn to relax.

The best way to relax is to learn to be grounded in the body. Progressive relaxation is something we can do anywhere. We have to familiarize ourselves with it again and again. We not only practice this as a way to prime the body and mind for meditation but also throughout the day. Whether in stillness or activity, this practice will transform the way we live.

I ask my students to incorporate this practice into their lives five times a day, even if only for a minute each time. I ask them to pick five times to do a progressive relaxation: every time they walk, are waiting in line somewhere, having the first bite of lunch, getting in an elevator, or at other specific times of the day. In other words, I ask them to pick five times to fully engage with the task at hand but to first start by relaxing from head to toe—to be fully in the body, feeling the skin, muscles, and tendons . . . and then relaxing them. Then they can be fully with the task. The more they do this, the more familiar they become with what it feels like to relax.

Relaxing our body brings the center of gravity down to our feet and makes us grounded. Tensing the body, on the other hand, brings our energy upward and causes us to be in our headspace—we become top-heavy. When the center of gravity is in the head region, we give rise to all sorts of problems like headaches and other physical issues. But the biggest problem with chronic tension is that it tends to make us controlling, activating our greed and aversion.

CONTROL

Tension, if left unchecked in meditation, influences the way we try to control the method. But we should not contrive when using a method. We allow the method to simply be present. The various attitudes and approaches to silent illumination I have discussed above lead to effortlessness and open awareness. By practicing in this way, we are staying with the reality of this present moment—free from the prison of old habits and erroneous views.

There's a special word in Chan for our controlling tendencies. It's called *guandai* in Chinese. The character *guan* means "control," but has the nuance of contrived effort. In modern usage, *guan* also means "management." The character *dai* means "to bind" or "to tie around," as in being tethered to something. The significance of this is that as soon as we try to control something, fixate on it, or make a contrived effort, we are tethered by it. Why?

Because we are going against the way things are, which is fluid and dynamic. If, for example, we have an emotion and we try to manage it by telling ourselves, "Don't think or feel that way; substitute this thought with that," then we will probably end up feeling worse because we are setting up an opposition and placing ourselves in a situation of conflict.

When we approach silent illumination by grounding the body, we're simply experiencing being here. What do I mean? We are aware of the act of sitting. How can we be aware that we are sitting here right now? There is the sensation of sitting, the presence of the body, the posture, the bodily weight of being here. We just relax into being here. Then all of these sensations are just present. If we reduce the present awareness to the simplest thing—the basic reality that there is a hunk of flesh and bones here—then this body and mind become inseparable from experiencing. Don't imagine that there is a mind observing the body like a corpse. This is not how to do it. The mind and body are here, together, inseparable. Their presence is effortless, noncontrolling.

The same is true of life. Someone may behave in a disrespectful or dismissive way toward us. We just experience the feeling of pain, the hurt, or unpleasantness. Even though it is our habit tendency to instantly solidify the feeling and make it into a "thing," we should simply allow it to be present without reacting to it or, even worse, allowing it to define us. If we make it into a thing, we separate ourselves from it and naturally oppose it. Self and other become solidified. This is the basis of suffering. Embracing the pain, we don't condemn either ourselves or the other person. We experience it as a natural human feeling that tells us something about ourselves. Then we can work with it and be in a better situation to respond and change the situation. If we're grounded, we notice things more. We see what underlies our feeling of hurt, what we are grasping.

Our need to control things can be seen in our relationships—for example, a parent-child relationship. Parents often feel the need to control their kids. They provide what is needed, and children either take advantage of the opportunities they're being offered, or they don't. If parents blame themselves for not teaching their children to take these opportunities, then they are creating unnecessary frustrations. We need to be able to discern the difference between our choices and our children's; we need to see the workings of causes and conditions. Each of us is merely one factor in the midst of all the complex workings of causes and conditions. We each have our own lives and karma, which we need to experience for ourselves. From our perspective, the choices our children make may not be so good, but that is only our perspective. Maybe they need to experience something challenging in order to be able to rise above it. When our kids become teenagers, it's best for us to relate to them as friends instead of as parents. We let them experience things themselves, but we're always there to support them when they need us. We try our best not to inject our own opinions into their lives.

The need to control is often seen in other kinds of relationships, such as romantic relationships. Very often people expect their partners to make them feel better or to take the pain away. They hang on to the partner, feeling they can't live without them: "You're my world," "You're my everything." Their whole lives revolve around that person. This not only puts a lot of stress on the partner, but at the same time, it is a form of self-denial because the person is defined through and objectifies the other as the source of happiness. Those relationships typically don't last because they are based on control and submission.

Control never works in relationships. It is the same with practice, because practice is a form of relationship. How we live our lives is replicated in how we practice. Some people, including teachers, practice with the aim of controlling their minds to be clear all the time. Moment to moment, they pay attention to every action, noting every detail, walking around like zombies—thinking that this is "mindfulness." They suppress their feelings and end up being lifeless and rigid. If we practice in this way, we perpetuate our tendency to control. This is just grasping and rejecting, the root of which is greed and aversion. Paradoxically, the more we strive in our practice, the more frustrated we get.

In practice, our awareness should not be intense but effortless, uncontrived. Our sense faculties are open, so they can do what they normally do while still being anchored in the body. Hearing sounds and seeing forms, we are grounded in the body without dwelling on any particular part of it. Various things may be perceived, but we're not swayed by them. Our experiencing is effortless because we're not trying to control the mind.

If you are the anxious or greedy type, you might think this is not enough. Your mind will jump around from here to there, seeking a "better" method. Being restless, you will come up with all kinds of ideas: "I'll check if my posture is correct—maybe it's better if I use another method...then I'll be able to get back to that good experience I had on the last retreat." Or, "Maybe I'm not relaxed enough...maybe I'm not using the method correctly."

Sometimes, on account of controlling habits, we develop a very subtle kind of grasping wherein we start holding our focus on a particular aspect of our sitting, perhaps a particular location in the body. Our focus is so constant that there comes a point where the rest of the body disappears. But unlike the natural disappearance of the body, which leaves us with an open, wakeful experiencing, this controlled concentration on a body part is something fabricated by the mind. That is, the object of meditation becomes static and unchanging, as opposed to vivid and dynamic. The mind has actually left its experience of the present moment and has slipped into sustaining a mental image of sitting or whatever we are fixating on. The original method is gone.

If we are fixing our mind on a concept, then we need to expose what's happening and return to the method. It is simple to do this, but we must do it and be careful, especially if we are the controlling type. Otherwise, we are just perpetuating our grasping. Not controlling means we're relaxed, nonchalant about the method. We are content and at the same time interested in the method.

Imagine holding a gemstone in the palm of your hand. You don't lose sight of it. It's there but you don't have to grip it tightly, fixating your gaze on it. You just let it rest effortlessly in your palm. Your awareness is resting on the gemstone, but not to the exclusion of everything else that is going on around you. You don't try to suppress other sounds in the room or other things that you see. It's just that your interest is resting on the gemstone in your palm. You can use the method like this.

The method brings us to the freshness of the present moment. Being with the present moment means not getting caught up with what we *think* it is, with what we *want* it to be or *make* it out to be. We are just experiencing the method right now, right here. Then mind, body, and the present moment become one—unified.

AWARENESS VERSUS SELF-CONSCIOUSNESS

Sometimes practitioners are confused about the difference between awareness and self-consciousness. This confusion arises because most of us are so used to our inner dialogue that we take it as awareness.

Self-consciousness is the habit of talking to ourselves, objectifying ourselves, sometimes even criticizing ourselves. "I shouldn't do this; I should be doing that." "Why is this happening to me? Why me?" "I'm not good enough; I wish others would see me." It's a self-referential mind, operating with a constant commentary. Self-consciousness is not necessarily bad; it is natural. Its function allows us to think, analyze, judge, and comment on what's going on within us and how we are doing in the world. So this ability to objectify ourselves is not really a problem in itself. The problem comes when we identify with these comments, turning against ourselves to criticize. This is not awareness.

We are conditioned by our family upbringing, our social networks and norms, and our own fixations. There's a reason why we are the way we are, and it has to do with the way we were raised, the way we were socialized and the things we learned from our parents, teachers, and so on. Buddhism also recognizes that we are the products of our actions (karma). Yet all of these experiences bring about a unique, individual path by means of which we can realize our true potential.

We can reflect on our actions in order to be more skillful, but we don't need to fixate on a critical self-narrative. In our introspection, we may recognize, "Wow, that was selfish of me; I should apologize and avoid doing that again." The thing is, we have to be conscious of why we are the way we are and make an effort to change. If we don't make a conscious decision, then we just continue to replicate our lives by following in the footsteps of our father or mother or those who have had an impact on us. We don't say, "Well, I'm just like this; actually, everyone is selfish. Why can't I be selfish too? I'm happier this way. I've got to take care of myself first, right?" We *should* be happy—it is our prerogative. But to be happy is not to limit ourselves to the same old narrative of me, I, and mine. We need to expose our habit patterns, embrace them, transform them, and let them go. The difference between introspection and self-consciousness is self-grasping.

Self-consciousness is different than awareness in practice. Awareness is more fundamental. It is an intrinsic quality of mind by means of which something can be directly experienced. It doesn't involve a running commentary, and, as such, it is different from self-narrative or self-criticism. In our meditation, we allow awareness to naturally *experience* our method of practice—without comments or judgments. We try to be 100 percent on the method.

When our awareness is deluded, it attaches to what we perceive—whether it is self or others—and may subsequently give rise to all sorts of mistaken notions and ideas. When awakened, awareness responds to situations effortlessly without reifying any perception—without self-reference. In our practice, we are focusing the mind so it engages with the method without giving rise to subsequent concepts or deluded thinking. In time, the experiencing awareness merges with the method.

Self-consciousness is quite common in meditation. Practitioners try to use the method in a contrived way, by talking to themselves while they are using it. For example, when strong emotions arise in meditation, they try to suppress them by saying, "Okay, let it go, let it go." But the emotions actually proliferate. This is because they are no longer using their method but rather have slipped into self-consciousness. Moreover, they have solidified their emotions into discrete ideas or narratives. Saying "let go" is not using the method. It's just being self-conscious, and so it doesn't work. We have to return to experiencing the method in order to be free from these passing emotions.

Awareness in practice is simply *experiencing* with openness. It is just being. Awareness is not something we have to fabricate—it is already here every moment. The key is to not allow awareness to congeal into ideas, concepts, and narratives. The second we reify awareness into a thing, it becomes self-conscious thinking, "Yes, my grief is terrible, and it's all because of him!" We're through—delusion has won. We're trapped in self-reference. So do not be attached. Keep awareness open, as it already is. The way to not solidify our experiencing is to have the right attitude. The way to cultivate the right attitude is to relax the body—to ground the method or whatever arises in the body. This means to embody the experiencing of each moment. The body is the anchor for experiencing. This is probably the most important element of practice. It's up to us to cultivate the right attitudes and relaxation, not only during meditation but in all aspects of life, because life itself is practice.

GHOST CAVES

A common pitfall for seasoned practitioners is dullness, a hazy state of mind, or some kind of fixation on stillness or a false experience of clarity. Whenever there is some kind of fixation, then we drop the method. Some take this stagnating, thoughtless mind to be samadhi or deep meditative absorption, but it is not. In Chan we call the various types of stagnation in stillness or clarity "dwelling on the dark side of the mountain in a ghost cave." No wisdom will come out of such states. Why? Because grasping is present.

Even serious meditators often perceive thoughts—no matter how subtle they may be—as the enemy. Because we tend to be repulsed by wandering thoughts in meditation, we focus on the stillness that arises and hold on to it. We may then try to lock our minds in the state in which thoughts are absent. Deep down, we think that this is the point of meditation—to have a mind free of thoughts. This is a misunderstanding of the principles of practice, and it is criticized by Huineng in the *Platform Scripture*:

> Good friends, the way must flow freely. How could it stagnate? When the mind does not abide in things, the way flows freely. When the mind abides in things, this is tethering yourself. If you say that always sitting without moving is it, then you're just like Shariputra berated by Vimalakirti.[1]

The "way" or the *dao* is awakening. The true nature of our mind is already free. It is only deluded when it is caught up with *things*. Attaching to states is to be caught up with things—including stillness. Huineng also states:

> In this teaching of seated meditation, one fundamentally does not fixate on mind, nor does one fixate on purity or stillness. If one is to fixate on the mind, then [one should know that] that mind is fundamentally a delusion. If you realize that the mind is like a phantasm, you also realize that there is nothing to fixate on. If one is to fixate on purity, then [one should know that because] our nature is fundamentally pure—it is through deluded thoughts that suchness is concealed. Just be without deluded thoughts and the nature is pure of itself.[2]

From the Chan perspective, fixating on a state of no-thought is a form of meditative absorption. Chan does not emphasize absorptions. Why? Because mind is not a *thing* we can fixate on. Our true nature is just *experiencing*, moment to moment—which is a fluid, natural, open wakefulness. It can't be used as a meditation object. Fixing on mind, purity, or stillness are just methods, constructs, expedient means to concentrate the mind so as to diminish wandering thoughts (clearing out the furniture) so the nature of mind can reveal itself (the room's spaciousness).

This is not a criticism of states of meditative absorption, since they are natural fruits of concentration practice. But Chan practitioners do not seek to experience them. The fact is, most practitioners are struggling with drowsiness, dullness, and other subtle forms of passivity, and all of these can become an object of attachment. The last thing they need is to chase after these states of stillness.

Sometimes in sustained meditation practice, we come to a fork in the road where the mind is settled with only a few subtle thoughts. At this juncture, two things can happen. First, the mind can slip into a hazy state where lassitude sets in. If we sit here for a long time, the method becomes vague and eventually the mind rests in the kind of dark state of nothingness or stagnation I mentioned above. No wisdom can ever occur here.

Sometimes the cause is bodily fatigue. Because we are generally conditioned or influenced by the body, when it is fatigued our minds become hazy. If we are seasoned practitioners, we may be able to sustain our posture for a long time due to years of practice. However, when we're in this state, we may be subtly moving our bodies—swaying—even when we don't recognize it. Our energy may also be very low. If we get used to this state, every time we sit we'll experience this low energy and its accompanying hazy state of mind. It is essential that we therefore do something about this—that we notice it at the onset and sharpen the mind right away by clarifying our method and resting our bodies if we are truly fatigued. Sometimes it may not be true fatigue but a habit tendency that has set in, so we must examine this closely. Left unaddressed, a hazy state becomes very difficult to uproot.

It is important to note that illusions and hallucinations may also appear at this fork in the road, and things buried deep in the unconscious may come up. One may see light or other phenomena. These are all what I consider scenery—not to be held on to, analyzed, or made into narratives.

A variant of this first fork of the road is a stale kind of stillness. It arises when there are no wandering thoughts, and we also let go of the method of meditation, something which should never happen intentionally. Because this state is so alluring and we're so captivated by it, we stop using the method and just rest in this stagnation. Of course, if we drop the method, that is the beginning of the end! The mind generally slips into a hazy state or eventually becomes scattered again. If it's the former, since we don't have too many wandering thoughts and the body is relaxed, we stagnate in dead stillness. This is not "silent illumination" because there is no freshness, illumination, or clarity.

Sometimes we take the stillness itself as the method. Creating a proximal state of no-thought, we then fixate on that. I've heard one teacher state that what he's doing is "illuminating the silence" by meditating on "the space between thoughts." This is also a mistake. This teacher has taken silent illumination literally, and has simulated a mental state of "silence" as an object. It is, of course, possible to make silence into a *thing*—this space between thoughts—and make it palpable, concrete. But it is just a mental construct. This created thing is a representation of a blank state of mind. We can certainly fixate on this object for a long time, and sometimes this state can be quite peaceful and alluring. We all want peace, after all. Our lives are chaotic and we want a respite from this chaos. So we seek it, but in doing so, we fabricate a false state. No wisdom can arise here. In most cases, subtle thoughts are still present—it's just that we have learned to ignore them. This is why the *Platform Scripture* states "that mind is fundamentally a delusion."

Less common is when we attach to a state of clarity and take it to be silent illumination. Because we so rarely experience this clarity, when it arises, our minds immediately attach to it. This is also the beginning of the end. Everything goes downhill from there. When clarity becomes a *thing*, it becomes dead—and because there's grasping of and craving for this clarity, it doesn't lead to genuine meditative absorption or wisdom.

The second thing or other fork in the road is when the person stays on the method and truly enters into meditative absorption, the experience of which is like a plane taking off. It takes a tremendous amount of concentration and energy but once it is airborne, it's smooth sailing. This momentum of concentration is fueled by the absence of desire; at the same time, the mind rests on the method without straying, achieving oneness of body and mind, then oneness of self and environment, then oneness of previous thought and subsequent thought. All thoughts are stilled, and the mind halts in the present. Meditative absorption is a natural state, and cannot be sought after. The seeking mind is diametrically opposed to this stillness. Desire agitates the mind. How can agitation lead to stillness?

There are, of course, many levels of meditative absorption. Without going into detail, suffice it to say that these absorptions are unified states of mind. When we come to this fork in the road, we should simply stay with the method of practice and ride it out. After we come out of a meditative absorption, we don't make a *thing* out of it.

Meditative absorption happens naturally as we sharpen the mind and stay with our method. As soon as a thought occurs, the power of awareness dissolves it—like a faint cloud vanishing in the sky. If we don't follow it, it simply vanishes. Practicing like this, concentration becomes strong and eventually unified. It's like a person riding a horse. The horse doesn't feel burdened by the rider; the rider doesn't feel awkward riding the horse. Together, they gallop. They become one. Is there a horse? Yes. Is there a rider? Yes. But they continue as one. This is the unified state. The momentum of concentration does not stop; it just continues as the energy of a single thought.

Still, meditative absorption, from the perspective of Chan, has the potential to become objects of attachment. For this reason, all of these states above are what the Chan tradition calls "being on the dark side of the mountain in a ghost cave." Why is it called a "ghost cave"? Because it is basically haunted by torpor, delusion, or absorption. A dark ghost cave is where the illumination of the sun doesn't reach. We get into this state because we either have not received proper guidance or have subtle attachments. Maybe we have never really practiced exposing the underlying tones of our mental states. We don't see the presence of subtle grasping or rejecting of thoughts. We are caught up with that which is experienced by the mind—instead of simply experiencing, which is the most natural way of being.

The antidote to these pitfalls is to recognize them and cultivate right attitudes in practice. But it takes a lot of effort to resist attachment to these states. I tell my own students to discontinue sitting for a while and do repentance prostrations instead, perhaps 108 prostrations a day. I tell them to repent for their karmic obstructions, which are caused by craving, aversion, and ignorance. When a person generates a sense of contrition and humility, self-grasping and stubbornness diminish, and this also diminishes the obstacles. They have to want to change in order to pull themselves out of these states, and sometimes this is hard because they are so peaceful and alluring. Lacking proper guidance, practitioners are likely to develop a habit of dwelling in these states.

WANDERING THOUGHTS

The opposite of the ghost cave is having scattered thoughts. We are linguistic beings, so thinking is natural to us. However, just because thinking is natural, it does not mean that we should let our thoughts run wild. That's how we become deluded in the first place—we become conditioned by thoughts and feelings. The way we think shapes our lives. Thoughts, subtle or coarse, dictate our choices and actions. So we have to be careful what we think, how we think. If we don't create a healthy relationship with our thoughts, if we are enslaved by them, then life will inevitably be hard.

How does meditation practice help us establish a healthy relationship with our thoughts? By going through the process of mental cultivation, we begin to expose our subtle thinking processes, learn to embrace them, work with them, and be free from them. It's like cleaning a room. If the room is cluttered, we can't do anything in it. If we clean the room, making it tidy and organized, we are able to work well; plus, we just feel more comfortable. That said, whether the room is clean and tidy or not, the room's spaciousness remains unchanged.

From the perspective of ultimate truth, we are originally awakened. Thoughts, good or bad, cannot affect our true nature. Clean or dirty, cluttered or vacant, our self-nature is not sullied by afflictions or thoughts. Still, from the perspective of conventional truth, we are often enslaved by thoughts. When we think sad thoughts, we're distraught; when things are going well and we're thinking happy thoughts, we're ecstatic. This shows that we're prisoners of our ever-changing thoughts. Besides, when our minds are cluttered, especially with self-referential thoughts, we have no control over how we feel. As I said before, we make life very hard for ourselves and those around us.

So we clean the room of clutter so we can experience the spaciousness of the room. Once we have gone through the process of self-cultivation and have cleaned our own room, we won't see thoughts as enemies. We won't be enslaved by them either. We will experience them as the natural expression of the mind, and we will be less likely to generate self-referential thoughts. Instead, our thoughts—and therefore our actions—will benefit those around us and will be appropriate for each situation. In addition, our wandering thoughts will diminish, and we will be clear and focused.

Some thoughts are beneficial and some not so much. But irrespective of what they are, if we're scattered, we can't accomplish anything. In general, the process of cultivation involves bringing the scattered mind to a concentrated mind; then from a concentrated mind to a unified mind; and from a unified mind we see through the nature of mind. In this process a method is of utmost importance. This process may sound linear, but it is not. Sometimes we may be scattered or tired, but after shifting our posture or approaching our method in a different way, we suddenly become clear and can use the method effectively. At other times, we may be using the method steadily and for no obvious reason—perhaps while hearing a sound or seeing an object—our self-grasping suddenly drops away.

Some people believe that a method is just another form of contrivance, so they prefer not to use any method at all. Usually those who take this stance don't really know what practice is about—they confuse a method with ideas about practice. Even a "methodless method" is a method without which the mind would be scattered. If we're unclear about our method, how can the mind be clear? How can the room be free of clutter if we don't clean it? Do we leave it to chance, magic, or faith?

When we use a method, we recognize the various types of wandering thoughts in our meditation so we can better work with the method. Any kind of thinking process that strays from our method of practice, away from the present, is considered wandering thoughts. These thoughts are mediated by the past or future or they are otherwise subtle reactions to the body or affected by the environment. In the present, there should only be the experiencing of the method. Thinking here includes both thoughts and emotions. Buddhism doesn't distinguish between the two—as stated earlier, both are forms of thoughts.

Wandering thoughts are those that take us away from our method. The first type is called scattered thoughts. These thoughts are random, fragmented, and without beginning or end; they have no underlying consistency. One thought may spark another seemingly unrelated thought and then that thought changes to another. These are mostly impressions from the day, mental activities that emerge from habit tendencies, and responses to what's happening in the present.

The second type of wandering thoughts is called discursive thinking. These thoughts are specific narratives that have a beginning and an end, or at least a process. Usually, they are things that weigh on our minds—a project that we need to finish, a trip that we have planned, and so on.

The third type of wandering thoughts are subtle thoughts. Thoughts don't arise devoid of feelings. There is always some sort of undercurrent feeling tone to these thoughts, however subtle, shaping our experience from one moment to the next. Subtle thoughts are not fully formed ideas, but are subtle moods or unconscious mental currents of our internal states. By "unconscious," I don't mean thoughts that were once conscious and were then suppressed, only to resurface again. I mean the activity that occurs outside of the realm of our everyday conscious mind. For example, sometimes we have an intuition, a flash of insight, while we meditate. These kinds of thoughts may feel spontaneous, but they usually emerge from an undercurrent of neural firings connecting with latent patterns that have been present in our unconscious for some time.

The undercurrents of our experience are encoded by countless subtle thoughts and feelings that group together, forming patterns. The more often these subtle thoughts cluster together, the more likely they associate together in the future. This is recognized in Yogachara as habit (tendencies or "seeds"; Skt. *vāsanā*), which shape our current perceptions by creating filters through which we experience what happens in the future. In this way, the habits we encode actually bias our ongoing perceptions and change the way we interact with ourselves and the world.

It is possible for us to expose all these different kinds of wandering thoughts, subtle or coarse, scattered or discursive, through training in meditation. To do this, we have to learn to relax into our bodies and familiarize ourselves with our bodily presence, then recognize the subtle shifts that we can make in the underlying tones of our internal states. The more we experience—the more we immerse ourselves with the subtle undercurrents of our internal states—the clearer we become.

As for which method we should use, it is best to work with a teacher. An experienced teacher will know which method is most suitable. In general, we start with a method that allows us to expose the workings of thoughts, such as meditation on the breath. Then, through sustained practice, and after we have developed some level of concentration, we move on to another method, one that is more in line with the principles of silent illumination as outlined in chapter 6.

PHYSICAL PAIN

When we are doing a seated meditation practice, we need to acclimate the body gradually to the meditation posture. There are several postures, but no matter which ones we use, if we engage in sustained practice long enough, physical discomfort will inevitably arise. There are several ways to deal with pain during meditation.

The first thing to do is relax. We must learn to relax the body, breathe naturally, and allow our minds to align with the right attitude so we can be clear. When we experience physical discomfort, it is usually in one area of the body—perhaps a knee or ankle. Maybe we feel pain in two areas, but rarely more. Examining this experience closely, we can recognize that each painful area is different. The sensations we're having and the quality of our discomfort are changing constantly. If we label it all as "pain," we are obfuscating the experience, applying a common label to a number of different sensations and thus shortchanging ourselves on our ability to apply our full awareness to them. Not only that, when we use the label "pain," we become more agitated. If we say to ourselves, "I'm having discomfort and it might get to the point where I can't stand it because we've only just started the sitting period!" then we are already lost in our heads. Usually, the *reality* is that there are sensations in only one part of the body that are attracting our attention.

That said, if pain is chronic, then we need to pay close attention to our posture, since a bad posture might be a contributing factor. If the pain is overwhelming, we might need to change our posture. In one sense, if we've gotten to that point, it's already too late. That sensation of pain is not cerebral anymore—stress hormones are flooding the body, we've gone into fight-or-flight mode, and since our bodies are tensing up around the pain, our attitude solidifies as aversion. Instead of letting this happen, we just change the posture mindfully.

If you become distracted by pain, then practice the following:

First, make sure the body is relaxed. Temporarily put aside the method. Put your awareness on the whole body and take some time to relax it from head to toe. Just as we learned to do when establishing a foundation of relaxation for practice, go through the whole body, relaxing each area as you go. Relaxing is important because you are short-circuiting the mechanism that causes the body to become tense and stressed.

Second, isolate the sensation. The whole body is not burning up. There's only one or maybe two areas that are uncomfortable. Don't exaggerate but do a reality check on what's happening. There may be sensations in the left knee that are different from the rest of the body; there may be a couple of other areas that are different. When it comes down to it, maybe there's only one area where you're experiencing discomfort. The rest of the body can still be relaxed.

Third, avoid the label "pain." We label out of habit, and the habit may have formed over years. We all have a long history with this body. When we label it as pain, we are applying an emotionally charged word to something that is just sensation. The word *pain* triggers a number of emotions and thoughts and mental images that carry us away from the actual experience of the body right here, in this moment. People sometimes start catastrophizing in these situations, telling themselves that they may be doing irreparable damage to their bodies if they don't move; that if they continue to sit they may end up never walking again. Our minds tend to get carried away with these dire proclamations. However, we might also remember that the pain often magically disappears as soon as we hear the bell ending the sitting period! What was excruciatingly real one minute melts into nothing the next. So how real was it? And we can also remind ourselves that when we have experienced intense leg or knee pain in the past, we've ended up being able to move around just fine after the sitting period was over.

Fourth, experience. What we are actually experiencing in this moment is changing sensation—just that. If the sensations are predominant and they are overpowering our method, then we can stay with the awareness of these one or two areas and be aware of the changing or different sensations. Don't label, just experience. What is it? Be open to it.

If we find that the pain is excruciating, then we just simply change the posture. It's not a big deal. It is best, however, to not move as a reaction. All of our lives, the way we have lived has been reactionary. So if we decide to change the posture, it is best if we do it slowly and mindfully, not in a reactive way. If we react, then it will be never-ending. We will be changing posture again and again and we will never be able to settle. So we move in a deliberate and relaxed way and, as we do so, we isolate the changing sensations. No words, no labels. We just watch the discomfort disappear or lessen in intensity. Then we can return to our original method.

Never make pain into a *thing*. Cultivate a state of vibrancy and wakefulness, not blocking anything. As in the analogy of the room, in the expanse of this room, which is the vast spaciousness of our mind, we allow things to be. The furniture is furniture, nothing else. If the furniture demands a lot of attention, if the chair has fallen over on its side and needs to be put upright, then we take care of it. We nourish it with our awareness, and it will be taken care of.

This concludes the discussion of what are the practical aspects of practice, covering right attitudes and methods in both formal meditation practice and daily life. Next, we will go into specific silent illumination teachings by Chan master Hongzhi. I have chosen three unique excerpts to bring out all the nuances of silent illumination and what practicing Chan means in daily life.

Part Two
Commentaries

PART 1 OF THIS BOOK lays out the foundations of Chan. In the three chapters that follow, I offer commentaries on selected passages from chapter 6 of Chan master Hongzhi's "Extended Discourse Records." These passages are the most relevant sections in Hongzhi's writings that pertain to Chan practice—its prerequisites, caveats, and stages. They also articulate the profundity of silent illumination, the degrees of experiential awakening, and the importance of post-awakening practice.

Mind has no stages. Awakening is intrinsic. However, due to the intensity of our own delusion, afflictions, and attachments, we experience stages and degrees. Hongzhi's writings talk about this but, because he tends to write allusively and poetically, it is easy to get lost in the beauty of his figurative language; the relevance of his words to practice may be lost. Worse, practitioners may take his words literally, *imagining* themselves experiencing those wonderful states of clarity or "silent illumination" while sitting in meditation. In my comments, I will bring his poetic words down to the level of our daily lives, showing how to apply them in practice.

I originally gave these commentaries during evening talks in a series of intensive Chan retreats. I've taught both beginner and seasoned retreatants, so these instructions address different aspects of practice, its psychosomatic states or "scenery," and the depth of initial awakening and post-awakening cultivation. You may find I reemphasize points discussed in the earlier chapters of the book, but in this context I come at silent illumination from different angles.

The titles of the chapters, which I added for convenience and to highlight the main thrust of each excerpt by Hongzhi, are mine. They do not appear in his original discourse record.

8. The Vacant Field

In the following excerpt, Hongzhi uses poetic allusions to talk about our intrinsic buddha-nature, both in its essence and function. He also articulates, from the perspective of practice, the nature of awakening and what the experience is like. But from the perspective of awakening itself, we are already whole and complete—the path is one of no-path; the mind that we hold so dear is one of no-mind.

> This vacant and open field is intrinsically present from the very beginning. You must purify and wipe away the various deluded conditioning and illusory habits. Naturally, you will arrive at a place that is clear and pure, perfect and bright. Totally empty, without any image, resplendent and outstanding, it does not rely on anything. Only this vastness can illuminate the fundamental reality as external objects are relinquished. Therefore, it is said, "With perfect clarity, there is not a single thing to be perceived." This field is where birth and death do not reach. It is the source of utter luminosity, able to emit light and respond clearly to the myriad dust motes [of sensory objects]. It is empty, without oppositions. The wondrous [activity] of seeing and hearing leaps far beyond those everyday sounds and forms. In all situations, its functioning is without trace; its mirroring is without obstruction. Mind and its objects naturally and spontaneously issue forth without partiality. An ancient said, "Having no-mind, one attains in oneself the Way of no-mind. Actualizing no-mind in oneself, the Way ceases to be." Advancing in such a way, you will be able to take up the responsibility [of helping sentient beings] with pure intent, as if you are sitting in perfect silence. As for the

wondrous activity of leisurely entering the world, it is something
you must investigate in this fashion!

From this passage, we can actually discern different aspects of practice. The
first two sentences establish the most important conviction about Chan
practice: that you lack nothing and you already have what it takes to awaken.
The "field" in this passage refers to your buddha-nature, or original freedom. Buddha-nature may be understood in terms of my analogy of the spaciousness of a room. Despite all the furniture that we tend to trip over, no
matter how cluttered or dilapidated these objects may seem, space is always
open—buddha-nature is ever present. This buddha-nature is not something
obtainable because it is not a *thing*. Nor can it ever be lost. It is an intrinsic
natural awakening. It is who you truly are—free.

Without this conviction, we can get caught up with different methods
of practice or different traditions of Buddhism—trying to determine which
one is better—or trying to attain some degree of spiritual accomplishment.
Why? Because many of us come to practice with a deep sense of lack, and
so we desperately need others to respect us or the teacher to validate our
insights. While we know that "there is nothing to attain," as clearly presented in the *Heart Sutra* or any of the other texts in the *prajnaparamita*
literature (a genre of Buddhist scriptures that focus on the teachings of the
perfection of wisdom), deep down we're always trying to chase after something or get somewhere. If we have some powerful experience and really
feel like we've attained something, then we can pretty much guarantee that
that's not an experience of seeing self-nature or awakening.

If a Chan teacher feels that they have realized "awakening," or that they
have authority over their students, then that so-called "awakening" is either
questionable or very shallow. Shakyamuni Buddha always said that he did
not lead the sangha—this is even less true of ordinary teachers! If a person
who has seen self-nature talks about it as something that is attainable, they
are just being silly. It's as though they were standing in water while everyone
else swims in it, and they start claiming, "Hey, I have realized what water is;
let me tell you how to find water." In fact, everyone is already swimming in
water. There's nothing special about water.

Unfortunately, people don't realize they're in water, just as they don't
realize they're already free. Instead, most people think they're suffering. So,
in response to the fact that we're already swimming in water, someone may
ask, "What do you mean? I'm not in water, I'm suffering; I'm in lava, not

water! I want to quench my thirst. Where's water?" In this case, it *is* up to the teacher to push that person's head down so they take in a few gulps and realize, "Oh, I'm in water!"

Sometimes we may have had a glimpse of self-nature but because our insight is not deep, that glimpse just remains a memory. Such experience has no transformative power at all. But when our insight is deep, then we no longer need to be persuaded about buddha-nature, and we don't think that our personal suffering—our agony, misery, and emotional affliction—is real. We realize that it is just a story.

Some of us are afraid of awakening. We may be practicing very well on retreat and then go to a personal interview with the teacher and say, "Teacher, I don't want to practice anymore." "Why? You are doing so well." "I'm afraid that if I get enlightened, my girlfriend won't recognize me anymore!" or, "I don't want to lose who I am." We think that awakening is some kind of vacant, empty nothingness in which we lose our memory or identity.

With awakening, we see through the veil of our identities, the stories, and the inhibitions. But we don't lose who we are. We still have our minds, our intellect, our memories, and the joy of life. It's just that for the first time we see the world without the colored lenses of self-reference. This construct of the self is based on a skewed self-image, erroneous notions, and dualistic thinking—precisely the things that create suffering in the world. As I said before, we can live just fine without "self" and we can be more productive, efficient, and in harmony with everything.

Isn't it true that we use events that happened to us to justify our own stories? That we see these events as a vindication of our beliefs? Sometimes we feel alienated, separate from the world out there. We see it as a world that needs to be escaped from, needs to be fixed; but that world exists only because of our self-attachment. The real world actually does not exist in the way we have imagined. This is why Shakyamuni Buddha said everyone is living in his or her own dream.

When the illusion of a separate, independent, permanent self is shattered, we will come to know that our fabrications and constructs are not an inherent part of us—they are not who we are.

Practice is not about awakening, for that is who we already are—this is the perspective of the awakened. From the perspective of the unawakened, practice is about eradicating delusion—our resistance to or disbelief about who we are. It's about seeing through all the bad habits that limit our potential to live fully. Thus, Hongzhi goes onto the next line: "You must purify and wipe away the various deluded conditioning and illusory habits." There are people who claim that Chan or Zen is not about "practice," or that there's no need. At best, these are just confusing perspectives. Worse, they are simply deluding themselves, especially if they are still conditioned by emotional afflictions and habit tendencies.

Even though we're intrinsically awakened, our conditioning prevents us from living our lives freely. This conditioning is made up of the ways we have learned to experience ourselves and others—the way we have learned to arrange the furniture in our room. If we encounter some other arrangement, we resist it: "That's not the way the furniture is supposed to go." Or we might start dividing it up: "This is *my* furniture and that's *your* furniture." Or, you may feel, "I'm sorry, you're right; I have no opinion—just put the furniture the way you like it." All of these are habits.

Some people have habituated themselves to be fighters while others are pushovers. The variety of our conditioning comes from lived experiences, but none of it is truly who we are. The furniture is not the room. Just because there are partitions or walls—even solid ones that have been built over many years, brick by brick—the space is unaffected by these walls. The fact that the wall can exist is due to the openness of the space. No matter how much we suffer, there is still opportunity to be free, to heal. We are incredibly resilient—if only we do not solidify and attach to our past. This, of course, does not mean we deny our past. But whatever our past may be, we allow ourselves to grow from it. How? We must "purify and wipe away the various deluded conditioning and illusory habits."

In the process of eradicating "deluded conditioning and illusory habits," it is very helpful to use the precepts to guide your actions; meditation to harmonize your body and mind; wisdom of no-self to dissolve emotional afflictions; and compassion to relate to others. Precepts are methods of practice, not commandments and rules. When you explore them, you will develop an appreciation for a stable life and come to realize more fully how your actions create the world in which you live. You observe your reactions when you are observing the precepts, and these reactions become indicators for your actions. That's the meaning of "purify."

With meditation practice, not only will you be able to do "housecleaning"—tidying up the furniture to make your room habitable, peaceful, and spacious—but with the help of precept observance your conditioning will start to unwind and deconstruct. This is the wondrous function of the three higher learnings of precepts, meditation, and wisdom. On the basis of them, your relationships with others will improve and your life will be much more stable and smooth. You will be able to sympathize with others and cultivate compassion. We call the essence of buddha-nature wisdom, and its function compassion. They are not two separate things. Wisdom and compassion are not even two wings of a bird. They are the same thing from different perspectives.

Hongzhi goes on to say:

> Naturally, you will arrive at a place that is clear and pure, perfect and bright. Totally empty, without any image; resplendent and outstanding, it does not rely on anything.

Is this the state of genuine awakening? No. It is merely scenery. It's a good scenery, and it may be quite attractive. If you don't practice, you will not experience anything like this, but such experience is not something to hold on to. Such a state is common for people who practice *shamata*, or calming meditation. This passage describes the utter clarity that practitioners experience in deep meditation states. Someone who experiences this state actually feels clear and empty. Is there a self? Probably. The self has become identified with the *feeling* of clarity and emptiness. Emptiness is not a feeling; it is not an experience. It is definitely not some kind of knowledge or idea. Experiences come and go; feelings are fleeting.

The surface meaning of this passage refers to what I consider to be an "approximation" of silent illumination. We may feel like we have seen our self-nature, but something is still there. As I said before, it's like looking through a clean window. We are able to see things so clearly, but there is still a window there! Similarly, when things are going well in practice, everything is great. But when interruptions come up or things don't go our way, this clear state will immediately vanish.

A deeper meaning of the passage refers to a realization of what premodern Chan texts call "the great death" of the self. It is a state where we have not come back to life yet—to the "great life." That is, we have experienced a lopsided, dead emptiness. That's why it is totally empty and without "image." This is not the emptiness of wisdom or prajna that is the lively functioning of selflessness. Instead, our small sense of self has died. The great self of unification still exists. Moreover, in this state we feel like we're invincible—"resplendent and outstanding"—like no one can touch us. We feel like we have truly experienced something. When we interact with others, we may seem very wise and compassionate, but what we're feeling is actually pity, as in, "How pitiable are those inferior practitioners." We feel we are above others.

There is a Chan axiom, "Illuminate the mind and see the self-nature." What the above passage points to is the stage of "illuminating the mind." But self-nature is not realized yet, so it's just half of the picture. In this state, there is just pure emptiness and clarity. It is something we've gained, something that keeps us separate from others. That's why it is "not relying on anything." True perception or realization of self-nature has nothing to do with the gaining of insight. It's silly to speak of it in these terms. "Look, I have a piece of paper, a certificate of dharma transmission." There's no need for recognition. When we interact with those who are awakened, there is no sense of self-aggrandizement at all. Genuine awakening is plain, down-to-earth. Nothing special.

Dahui, one of the greatest Chan masters, experienced this in his twenties. His teacher was Yuanwu, who also taught Hongzhi. One day, Yuanwu said to Dahui, "Haven't you seen how the southern breeze comes along and the wisteria in the north starts to shake?" That's like saying, "A slaps B in the face, but C feels the pain on his cheeks." Upon hearing this, Dahui suddenly dropped his self-attachment. He was in this state of emptiness. Yuanwu recognized this but didn't give him the seal of affirmation of awakening, or *inka*. Dahui had illuminated his mind of emptiness but he hadn't yet come alive. He had not realized the perfect functioning of selfless wisdom.

Some teachers like to give out affirmations of awakening, or *inka*, and "dharma transmissions," so they'll have more disciples. Thank goodness Yuanwu didn't approve of Dahui's experience—that would have ruined Dahui's wisdom life! It was only after numerous such experiences and more powerful insights that Yuanwu finally verified Dahui's awakening.

> Only this vastness can illuminate the fundamental reality, as external objects are relinquished. Therefore, it is said, "With perfect clarity, there is not a single thing to be perceived." This field is where birth and death do not reach.

What is genuine awakening, or seeing self-nature, our buddha-nature? How does one "come back to life"? By letting go of "awakening," or whatever attainment or quasi awakening we feel we've had. Hongzhi expresses this as "vastness." Here, vastness refers to complete openness, receptivity, and the dropping away of self-reference. Only then will we be able to "illuminate intrinsic reality and relinquish external objects." Intrinsic reality refers to buddha-nature, which is just the nature of emptiness, no-self. "External objects" are those which oppose the self. Of course, there is no self to speak of in Buddhism. But we feel there is a subject (me) and there is an object outside of me. This is what is meant by objects opposing the self.

When self is dropped, our sense of others and world "out there" is also relinquished. Do others and the world exist? Of course, but we no longer experience them in opposition to us. That's why "there is not a single thing to be perceived." Yet, in awakening everything exists—it's just that the self doesn't. In this state, birth and death are transcended.

> It is the source of utter luminosity, able to emit light and respond clearly to the myriad dust motes [of sensory objects]. It is empty, without oppositions. The wondrous [activity] of seeing and hearing leaps far beyond those everyday sounds and forms. In all situations, its functioning is without trace; its mirroring is without obstruction. Mind and its objects naturally and spontaneously issue forth without partiality.

With the self out of the way in our relations with the world, all things truly come alive. When all things come alive, there's no beginning or end—just the miraculous functioning of selfless wisdom acclimating to different situations. Being empty, we are able to respond to everything without the filter of me, I, and mine. That said, even though we may be awakened, our ability to help others is still limited. Hence, there's a need for post-awakening practice. How do we do this?

There are three kinds of wisdom—or awakenings—in Buddhism. These are: fundamental wisdom, experiential wisdom, and acquired wisdom. Fundamental wisdom refers to our buddha-nature, our intrinsic freedom, our natural awakening. Experiential wisdom refers to the dropping away of our self-reference, namely actual awakening, and this has to happen again and again. Our emotional afflictions, habits, and self-grasping are so strong that even when we have a genuine awakening experience, self-grasping eventually returns. So people who have had genuine awakenings are actually humbled by their own self-grasping in daily life. Practice continues and they work on their afflictions and self-grasping and gradually mature their insights. Acquired wisdom refers to post-awakening cultivation. It also refers to the wisdom of expedient means. It is a wisdom that helps others and, at the same time, grinds away all of our sharp corners—habit tendencies and emotional afflictions—and brings to fruition our full potential.

On the subject of expedient means, it needs to be said that only great bodhisattvas are able to truly exercise expedient means. This is acknowledged in all Mahayana scriptures. Ordinary practitioners and teachers can only subdue the emotional afflictions that lie dormant; they cannot eradicate them yet. Subtle afflictions and habits are the different forms of craving, aversion, and ignorance, referred to in Hongzhi's text as "trace" and "obstruction." The last traces of these afflictions are only relinquished just prior to full buddhahood. When great bodhisattvas exercise the true wisdom of expedient means, it truly benefits and transforms people. For example, these expedient means bring about awakening and insight in others. Teachers who claim they are using expedient means but actually abuse and bring about pain in their students are simply delusional.

Post-awakening practice for ordinary practitioners is simply making ourselves available, without reservation, to all people and all aspects of life. Life truly comes alive as an arena for cultivating the six bodhisattva *paramitas* or "perfections": generosity, morality, patience, diligence, meditation, and wisdom. Only through interacting with the complexity of life, with all of its ups and downs, among people, is selfless wisdom able to truly fulfill its potential. This is why these six are called perfections.

If we don't meet annoying people, how are we able to cultivate patience? Unless someone else pushes our "buttons" or gets under our skin, how would we come to know that these buttons are there? If we don't confront complex human relationships, how are we able to know the depth and skillfulness of precepts? If we don't come across people in need, how will we know what generosity means?

Chan has a saying, "the responsiveness of wisdom is like two arrows meeting in midair," meaning we are able to function aptly or appropriately. It is like a cup with a perfect lid. Have you seen those toys for children between two and three years old that have different shaped pegs? Children have to put the pegs into the appropriate hole. There are round pegs for round holes, triangular pegs for triangular holes, and so forth. The kids have to figure out which peg goes where. At first, they try to squeeze the square into the triangle or circle but gradually, by trial and error, they learn. Post-awakening practice or acquired wisdom is like this—we meet different people or situations that provide us with the opportunity for practice. Concretely, this means not injecting our "selves" into the situations in which we find ourselves. Doing so would be like trying to fit a square peg into a round hole.

Those who have had genuine awakening experiences are different from those who have never experienced awakening. The power of their experience lingers even though their self-grasping returns. They are acutely aware when their self-grasping is present. To them, it sticks out like a thorn. They see it in the subtle underlying feeling tones, in the way they behave in certain situations and in their conversations with others. This may be hard for ordinary people to understand because all that they've ever known are self-referential thoughts, feelings, actions, and conversations. In concrete terms, not injecting a "self" into life situations means not seeing these situations through the lens of gain and loss, fame and humiliation, praise and blame, joy and sorrow. In Buddhism, these are called the "eight winds" and they can blow us off our feet, whirling us around from here to there, up and down. Actually, there are more than eight winds. In the *Platform Scripture*, Huineng speaks of thirty-six pairs of opposites that plague us all the time. It's not that we go looking for these situations but, as long as we engage in life, they will come up. As long as there are people, they will come up—at work, at home, even in temples.

When we don't inject ourselves into the situation yet we fully engage with others, we are able to cultivate wisdom in daily life. Hongzhi expresses this as:

> In all situations, its functioning is without trace; its mirroring is without obstruction. Mind and its objects naturally and spontaneously issue forth without partiality.

The mirror has no fixed images. Does it respond? Yes, it responds, not for its own sake but for the benefit of whoever stands in front of it. Acquired wisdom responds to the needs of sentient beings. This is genuine compassion that flows forth naturally and is precisely what sentient beings need. After awakening, there's no need to say, "I have to save sentient beings." This is dualistic thinking. We just do it. Do you understand? The selfless "mirror" is empty. Precisely because it is empty, it responds perfectly, but in its reflection there is no self.

In the *Vimalakirti-sutra*, Manjushri asks Vimalakirti, "How should a bodhisattva regard sentient beings and all of their actions?" Vimalakirti replies, "Bodhisattvas should regard sentient beings as the moon in the water, reflections of a mirror—empty, like a dream."[1] At the same time, bodhisattvas should generate an impartial compassion to help all beings. So while this world is full of suffering, suffering is an illusion and comes from delusion. Even though sentient beings are like reflections in the mirror, we nonetheless offer ourselves for their benefit. In this process of engaging with the illusions of vexation and suffering, we realize awakening. From emptiness comes action, and through our actions we recognize emptiness. If a mirror has a permanently etched image, whatever it reflects will be skewed, juxtaposed against it. It won't be clear. Similarly, our actions will surely be skewed if we're driven by our self-referential agendas.

In Buddhism, emptiness is not vacuity, nor is it a thing. It is made up of relationships and connections. So engaging with the world means we must know how to work with relationships and not be so fixed and inflexible. We must know how to respond to those around us without projecting our self-referential concerns so that whoever we're interacting with may "naturally and spontaneously" be while we remain without partiality.

Hongzhi continues by citing an earlier Chan master's words to express the idea of not injecting one's "self" into situations in daily life:

> Having no-mind, one attains in oneself the Way of no-mind.
> Actualizing no-mind in oneself, the Way ceases to be.

No-mind doesn't mean no mental activity. It's a pre-Buddhist Chinese expression of effortlessness and unpretentiousness for one who cultivates the Way or the *dao*—you may say it's the way of the Daoist sage. Chan masters appropriated this existing idea to express selfless wisdom. "No" here means no self-reference; "mind" here includes both mind and heart, thoughts and feelings. It's the same idea as the empty mirror reflecting images. For most, all of our thoughts and feelings are mediated by self-reference. So no-mind here is just another way to say the wisdom of no-self.

"Attaining" here in Chinese consists of two characters: *ti*, which means both "experiencing" and "embodying," and *de*, which means "obtain" or "realize." In Chinese, experiencing and embodying are intertwined—body and mind are one. Experience is not a cerebral thing; it must be embodied. Chan awakening is expressed in the verb form "experiencing-embodying." So grammatically, *ti* and *de* function in the infinitive form. The language points to the fact that actualizing is not a static experience but a continual process of experiencing and embodying. Again and again, we have to not inject our self-reference in all situations of life. This is to realize the Way.

As Hongzhi says:

> Advancing in such a way, you will be able to take up the responsibility [of helping sentient beings] with pure intent, as if you are sitting in perfect silence. As for the wondrous activity of leisurely entering the world, it is something you must investigate in this fashion!

After the awakening of selfless wisdom, how do we relate to sentient beings? What makes our intent pure is the lack of self-reference—not injecting and projecting one's own attachment or ideas onto them. To do this, Hongzhi advises us to be "leisurely." This is what I call the right attitude of contentment: being at ease, relaxed, and without contrivance. To contrive is to inject a self where there is no need for one. Also, contrivance always manifests as self-consciousness which, as we saw, is different from awareness. Many people practice with self-consciousness, criticizing themselves or constantly judging and commenting on how they're doing. This is not leisurely. Get rid of self-consciousness! We may introspect and improve our conduct if that is the task at hand, but we don't need to sabotage the present moment with a running tape about ourselves.

Be in the moment, be one with whatever you're doing. A Tang dynasty Chan master, Banshan Baoji (eighth century), once said, "Like the earth that holds up a mountain, unaware of its steepness and loftiness; like the stone that contains jade, unaware of its flawlessness."[2] The stone contains the jade. Perhaps Westerners aren't into jade. Diamond might be better. A coal block contains the diamond, yet there is no self-consciousness of ordinariness in coal or preciousness in the diamond. People who mine the diamonds judge them as precious. It is people who consider coal as ordinary. Similarly, awakened persons do not perceive themselves as holy. The deluded perceive them as such.

Buddhadharma has no high or low, no barriers or insights, no stages of practice. But when we practice in delusion, a path unfolds, and high and low, barriers and insights, and stages appear. All these appear because of our discriminations. Yet we must practice just to practice, with the attitude of leisureliness. A teacher teaches just to teach. Students get the benefit, but the merit is all theirs. A teacher doesn't think, "Am I not great? Gosh, I'm so helpful to people." That would be creating a self where there isn't one. To practice "leisurely" is to practice selflessly. This is the only way to continue our practice before and after awakening.

This may be a lot to digest, but having the right understanding of practice and awakening, slowly bringing ourselves to it, little by little we will find that the dharma becomes alive in us. Our relationship with practice, with the world, with what appear to be obstacles, will start to change. And then we'll realize what Chan master Yunmen has said; "Every day's a good day!" Or, as I say, "It's all good!"

9. THE INVESTIGATION

CHAN PRACTICE can be said to be an investigation of our true color. How do we investigate it? What does it take? Typically, among Zen people the word "investigate" is associated with the *huatou* or *gong'an* (Jpn. *koan*) method of practice, but this word has a much broader significance. The Chinese characters for "investigate" here are *tijiu*, which Hongzhi often used to describe the process of cultivation.

Ti means "embodying" and *jiu* has the connotation of "thoroughness," or "thorough penetration." In modern usage, *jiu* means "research," but this is not how it was used in premodern classical Chinese; rather, it meant "experiencing something thoroughly." Hongzhi couples these two characters to mean "thoroughly embodying this investigation." What should we as practitioners thoroughly investigate? Our true color. Here's how to do it:

> Unpretentious and empty, pure and still, cold and dispassionate, innocent and genuine—this is how to eradicate countless lifetimes of accumulated habit tendencies. The moment habit tendencies and defilements exhaust themselves, intrinsic luminosity will manifest, blazing through your skull. Vacant of external things, cleansed and spacious—like the merging of the sky and the autumn lake. Like the sameness of the snow against the winter moon. This field has no horizons or boundaries—it cannot be measured. When it is experienced as one vast expansive continuity without any sharp corners or seams, you must thoroughly relinquish this [experience]. This relinquishing is not something that can be conceived of or theorized about through discursive reasoning. How can it be gained through any instructions or comments? Only one whose bottom of the barrel has fallen off can be convinced of this. Thus, it is said, "Only by actualizing it

would one be in accordance with it." To be in accordance with it is to enter the world to roam and play in samadhi, where everything manifests as it is. Sounds and forms, shadows and echoes are engaged with directly, yet none of them leave any impressions or traces. In the midst of it all, it is as if there have never been interactions or responses. Not being subjected [to form], you will embrace the myriad forms and appearances in the vastness of *dharmadhatu*. There will not be any outflows whatsoever. Person of true color, investigate this in this fashion.

"True color" is a Chan expression for buddha-nature, our intrinsic awakening. It has nothing to do with skin complexion or race. A person of true color is one who is awakened. Ultimately, to realize our true color is why we engage in practice, to be free from the shackles of delusion and see our self-nature. Ordinary people may not realize this, but what lies behind their feeling of unhappiness is the existential dilemma of not knowing who they are, their true color.

There are many Chan expressions that probe our true color: "What is your original face?" "If all things return to the one, where does the one return to?" "Who is this person without rank?" These are called *huatou*, or critical phrases. Literally, *huatou* means the "source of spoken words," or that which is before concepts or ideas, thoughts and feelings. What is it?

To practice Chan or Zen is to investigate your existence, your true nature. The question is how to investigate it. You can't use words or language—these are precisely the cause of your entanglement and anguish. As a being who uses language, words and labels shape your feelings about yourself and your experiences of the world. Perhaps you've been told—or you've told yourself as you compared yourself to others—that you're rich or poor, beautiful or ugly, skinny or fat, useful or worthless. You have been swayed by these ideas, taking them for who you are. You have mistaken these descriptors as reality and based your actions around them, forming habits, toiling and striving without end. Suffering.

The way out of suffering is to regain your true color, your original face. How? By thoroughly embodying the investigation of Chan—by practicing! Hence, the text says, "Only by actualizing it would one be in accordance with it." You must go beyond words, language, emotional afflictions, and habits. Thoroughly decondition yourself.

> Unpretentious and empty, pure and still, cold and dispassionate,
> innocent and genuine—this is how to eradicate countless life-
> times of accumulated habit tendencies.

Hongzhi, with his grandmotherly heart, spells it out: To practice is to be "unpretentious and empty," face your afflictions and habit tendencies and work with them. How? Purify them, still them; be "cold and dispassionate" to them. Eventually you will be able to let go of them, and your life will then be freer, happier. This is to be "innocent and genuine" and it is the way to "eradicate countless lifetimes of accumulated habit tendencies."

Some practitioners are pretentious, arrogant. Instead of being empty, they have read a lot and have a lot of notions floating in their heads. Then they imagine they are experiencing them in their practice, believing themselves to be advanced practitioners.

One time, a person came to our center. Supposedly he had been practicing Vedanta, Zen, all kinds of stuff, for many years. I gave a dharma talk, and he asked a question about non-dual clarity, but his question went on for a few minutes. Obviously, it wasn't a question at all; he just wanted to express his knowledge and get some kind of affirmation of his realization. As he was asking his so-called question, a beautiful woman stood up in front and walked across the room to go to the bathroom on the other side. As he was talking, his eyes were following her. I was sitting in front of him and I said, "Hello, I am here!" He continued to talk about those fancy words like "bare attention," "non-duality" and so on. When he finished, I said, "So, did you have a moment of non-dual awareness of the woman you were watching?"

As long as you still attach to forms, don't talk yourself into believing that you're not attached. If there's form in your mind, you need to observe precepts. You have to not react to your attachments to form, but first you need to expose your attachments, then you can practice being "unpretentious and empty." People who are pretentious don't even see themselves as pretentious. Their minds are turned to the world instead of to themselves. Most have no ability to distinguish between their thoughts about something and the thing itself—they think what they think *is* the object. They have mistaken the descriptor as reality. These are called outer path practitioners.

Outer path practitioners practice externally; even if they think they're cultivating the mind or have had some powerful experience, they're objectifying everything as a *thing* they possess. Buddhadharma or the Chan path is the inner path. There's no attainment, no wisdom, no mind outside this moment. Because there's no attachment, we realize great wisdom that frees ourselves from fixations. We are at peace, and the joy from unloading our burden of afflictions is indescribable.

Practice is not about denying your past but exposing or facing it, embracing it, working with it, and being free from it. There is a history to the way you are, and you need to work with your issues. This is a fourfold process, discussed in chapters 2 and 3, and it is not linear but reciprocal. The more you are able to expose what's happening inside you, the more you are able to accept yourself. The more you are able to embrace yourself, the more you actually see. The more you see, the more likely you are able to let go. The problem is we don't usually look inside; we look outside for the answers. The truth is, only we know how we feel, why we feel the way we do, and what we can do to change it. Most of the things that drive us are habits.

Habit tendencies are something we have to repeatedly expose, embrace, transform, and let go. We have to continuously work on them because they come back again and again through different guises. Practice is a journey and we're taking all of our emotional afflictions, all of our habit tendencies, along. It's like taking our babies with us on a trip. One baby may be greedy; another may be angry all the time; another may be grumpy; still another may have a deflated self-worth. Each day, our babies grow and mature; they grow with us. We have to teach the children we have within. We definitely don't want to ignore them or deny their existence. That will only make things worse.

Recently a man came to a series of classes I did on the *Vimalakirti-sutra*. He challenged everything I said. At the end he said, "I used to practice but I was miserable. So now having given up practice, I am so much happier. I have fully accepted who I am and the fact that there's nothing I or anyone else can do to help me. No one can help anyone else." When I heard that, I just smiled. Have you met people like that? I then said to him, "Why are you here, then?" he said, "I don't know, I *feel* like it." People are often pushed and pulled by their own feelings and ideas, like a puppet on strings. They have absolutely no autonomy. Actually, what this man really wanted was to be seen, to be heard, and to be loved. After chatting with him after class, I discovered that what he considered "practice" in his earlier life was just suppression. He had tried very hard to deny his afflictions, ignore, and "let go" of them. He used buddhadharma as a measuring stick to gauge himself. That's why he was so miserable. This is a common problem.

Usually people only know how to grasp or reject. They don't realize that grasping and rejecting are the poisons of the mind, so the more they practice, the more they suffer. We have to treat our emotional afflictions and habits as our own babies. When your babies cry, do you dismiss them and walk away? No, you have to hug and soothe them. Practice is a relationship. You have to cultivate the right attitudes in this relationship. You can use your own habit tendencies of grasping and rejecting to deal with habit tendencies.

The right attitude is non-grasping, non-rejecting—contentment. That is, "unpretentious and empty, pure and still, cold and dispassionate, inno-cent and genuine." These words describe the important principle of non-opposition we must practice when faced with habit tendencies. This doesn't mean we give into them or follow them. It means we expose them—we have to first see them as they arise. If we don't even see them, we will definitely follow them. The man who came to my classes saw his vexations, but in his "practice" he tried to fight them, to reject them. That's why he was so mis-erable. In his delusion, he then just let his practice go and gave into those vexations. And he thought that doing so made him happier. Have you ever felt this way? If you have, then you must expose this attitude of giving up because that's just the flip side of grasping.

The way to practice is to expose, accept, and not react. This is the mean-ing of "pure and still, cold and dispassionate." Dispassionate doesn't mean disinterested. As we saw, one of the key attitudes is to be interested—fasci-nated—but at the same time nonreactive. That's how to be "innocent and genuine." Why is it called innocent? Because it is without contrivance. This is being genuine to our true nature, which is free of afflictions and habits.

In Chan, there's an expression of distinguishing "host and guests." The host is our intrinsic awakening. The guests are adventitious afflictions and habits. Please don't confuse who's the host and who are the guests in your house. If you do this, things will be upside down. That is unfortunately how some people live their lives, and that's why the *Heart Sutra* says, "Having no obstructions, there is no fear—departing far from upside-down thinking and imagining."

Emotional afflictions and habits hide in the shadows. They lurk behind and meddle with every moment of our waking and sleeping hours, so the first step we need to take is to turn on the light. Don't suppress them; just expose them right when they arise. This means you see what is happening and you're clear about it. Be honest with yourself and take responsibility—whatever you feel is yours. Don't blame others. Transform your afflictions and habits. Redirect their energy to relax your body. Tension is the fuel line for afflictions—we have to put a crimp in the fuel line by relaxing. If you really must redirect your thinking, then, if stinginess arises, see whatever you possess as having no owner; if craving or desire arises, see it as a chance to recognize the purity of mind; if frustration arises, see it as a free session to practice patience; if laziness arises, see it as a way to exercise diligence; if scattered thoughts arise, see the mind that is originally devoid of thoughts; if self-centeredness arises, then see it as a mirage. This is the way to practice the six perfections: generosity, morality, patience, diligence, meditation, and wisdom.

Buddhism provides alternative ways of relating to ourselves and the world. Because we're upside down, we have to make things right side up again. The most direct approach in Chan practice is not to even entertain any antidote to counter afflictions. Simply expose and embrace them. Not responding to them is itself transforming and letting go of them. If we cannot do this, then we can use the different means listed above to work with our afflictions.

> The moment habit tendencies and defilements exhaust themselves, intrinsic luminosity will manifest, blazing through your skull.

Self is already empty; awakening is intrinsically complete. There is no need to seek awakening or "intrinsic luminosity" outside yourself. Don't try to realize some miraculous, wondrous state of selflessness. Don't try to fabricate a self. There's originally no-self. Why would you want to create a self and then eradicate it? Note, however, that Hongzhi never denies habit tendencies. He doesn't say they are nonexistent. Even though everything is empty and there's no-self, there are real consequences to emotional afflictions and habit tendencies. This is the view of Chan.

So do we have to wait until *all* habit tendencies and defilements exhaust themselves before intrinsic luminosity manifests? No. It doesn't work that way. This is why the text says: "The moment habit tendencies and defilements exhaust themselves." "The moment" means "at the time."

Earlier I spoke of three kinds of wisdom: fundamental, experiential, and acquired wisdom. Experiential awakening is what practitioners talk about, and it refers to selfless wisdom. If experiential awakening is deep enough, emotional afflictions and habit tendencies vanish. As soon as they vanish, our true nature or "intrinsic luminosity" manifests. However, these afflictions and habit tendencies are not really eradicated. Self-grasping eventually comes back. That's why we have to continue to work with our afflictions. Even for thoroughly awakened masters, subtle habit tendencies are still present. It's just that they lie dormant—they don't manifest. It is said that only great bodhisattvas, just shy of full buddhahood, are free from these subtle forms of ignorance.

In practice, just deal with your garbage. There is no denying that what you do, how you think, affects others. You only need to stop and reflect to see that this is true. No one lives in a bubble. Everyone is connected in some way. Thus, practice continues and experiential awakening deepens.

> Vacant of external *things*, cleansed and spacious—like the merging of the sky and the autumn lake. Like the sameness of the snow against the winter moon. This field has no horizons or boundaries—it cannot be measured. [Italics are mine.]

In experiencing awakening, there is no inside or outside, self or others. This is why it's "pure." But this purity is not in opposition to defilement. It is the absence of both purity and defilement. That's why it is pure. Dualistic notions only exist when there is self-centered thinking. When self-centeredness is present, everything is ruined. Even when something wonderful happens, because your anticipation or expectation of it is different, it appears sour. However, when self is absent, as it always has been, everything is "cleansed and spacious."

In awakened activity, there is no separation. You don't make people into "others," into *things*, projecting onto them a permanent essence of some sort. With this, there's just this; with that, there's just that. Selfless wisdom is present for all, yet everything is distinct. For this reason, the text says, "Like the merging of the sky and the autumn lake. Like the sameness of the snow against the winter moon."

Have you seen the horizon where the sky meets the ocean? The two seem like one, blending into each other. Or maybe you can appreciate fresh snow on mountain peaks against the winter moon? They're the same color. These beautiful images exhibit the wonder that exists in awakening when the self is absent. But the same is true when you witness an argument among people or stand at a busy intersection—they are just like the horizon where the sky meets the ocean or the snow against the winter moon. There's an indescribable peace and openness in all of it: a wondrous dialogue of give and take, push and pull, alive and fresh, instant by instant. Yet from the awakened person's viewpoint, it is as if nothing is happening. All things are fluid—nothing is reified. That's why the text says, "vacant of external *things*." Your mind is not agitated, nor is it separate from all that's happening around you.

The text continues:

> When it is experienced as one vast expansive continuity without any sharp corners or seams, you must thoroughly relinquish this [experience]. This relinquishing is not something that can be conceived of or theorized about through discursive reasoning. How can it be gained through any instructions or comments? Only one whose bottom of the barrel has fallen off can be convinced of this.

This passage is for those who are experienced in practice and have had some insight. Just because you may have experienced awakening doesn't mean the task is over. Genuine practitioners have a sense of humility. They do not put on airs or present themselves as better than others. Far from it. Being down to earth, they are perfectly fine mingling with all kinds of people and are able to just take the back seat. Why? Because they realize their own afflictions are like "sharp corners" hurting others; they work on themselves to make sure there are no "sharp corners or seams." People get hurt by sharp corners. Seams are gaps. Practice shouldn't have gaps and fissures. It should be continuous. This point is where true practice begins. After some insights, you see what needs to be done—you see exactly how the illusory self works, how it gives rise to afflictions, and how your actions are habitual.

Some seasoned practitioners and teachers are smug. They're perfectly compassionate and caring when they help beginning practitioners, but before other teachers or their peers, they have to show how experienced they are.

My teacher had a student like that. We shared teaching duties at the center when my teacher was away. He was always helpful to newcomers and he liked to take the lead in everything. I was fine with it because some of the things he said to students were useful, as he was experienced in practice. However, he always had a thing about authority figures. He even started to criticize and challenge my teacher for sanctioning other students who had had experiences of seeing self-nature. He thought no one was on a par with him. And even though my teacher wasn't authoritarian by any means, the student always had an opinion about the things he said. In fact, he was dissatisfied with every teacher he encountered or studied with. No one was good enough. His critical mind was overbearing. He had set up an ideal of how teachers should be only to find faults and errors with them. He filtered everything through his habit tendencies so, while he was kind to beginners, his true colors showed when he was among peers and teachers. It was quite sad. For his part, my teacher accepted the student as he was. No matter how critical he was, my teacher accepted him. Eventually, this student left the center.

Awakening experiences, along with insights and any other experiences, must be forgotten. Practice must continue. Genuine practitioners hold nothing back. They are thorough and clear. This ability is not something for which knowledge and intelligence can substitute. Hence, "this relinquishing is not something that can be conceived of or theorized through discursive reasoning."

Do you want to hold on to your cherished awakening experience? Or are you going to let it go? To let go, you have to expose it, accept it, and work through it. No one can do it for you. It is something that you must do yourself. There are no "pointers or instructions" at this point. Seasoned practitioners should know already what needs to be done.

The "bottom of the barrel falling off" is a Chan analogy for thorough awakening. If we hold on to our past awakening experiences—which is like punching holes through the bottom of the dark barrel—we will never know what true freedom is. Even though some light is able to shine through, some parts of the barrel remain dark. For thorough awakening to take place, the whole bottom of the barrel must fall off.

> To be in accordance with it is to enter the world to roam and play
> in samadhi, where everything manifests as it is.

For those who have had insights and awakenings, it is important that they engage with the world. Only in the midst of chaos and turbulence will their hidden emotional afflictions and habit tendencies manifest. Experiencing the pain of losing those you love, dealing with aggression and discrimination, interacting with authority figures and helping those in need, taking up positions of power, all of these are the playground of a Chan practitioner.

To genuinely be in accordance with our true nature, to manifest our full freedom in wisdom and compassion, we must "enter the world to roam and play in samadhi." This is a wonderful expression. Some people have lofty ideas about entering the world and saving all beings. But it can be dangerous. If we don't know what we're doing, we don't "roam and play." Instead, we end up being *played* by all our samsaric tendencies.

Practice is difficult, no doubt about it. But it's the only way. If we don't practice in daily life, we will never know what practice is about. Living in a cocoon, we may think we're free and at ease, but in reality all our emotional afflictions and habits are just hidden and, if we do engage with the world, we will inevitably hurt ourselves and others with our actions, speech, and intentions. To practice in the world is the only way to be free, bring out our resilience, and truly benefit others.

> Sounds and forms, shadows and echoes are engaged with directly,
> yet none of them leave any impressions or traces. In the midst of
> it all, it is as if there have never been interactions or responses.

Emotional afflictions arise mostly through sounds and forms—what we see and hear, especially in our interactions with others. I have a lovely student who can't seem to work with others. Whenever there's a group project, few want to collaborate with her. They don't get her. She preemptively sees potential flaws and problems in every detail. "This is not good enough because it's flawed." "If we use that product, we will all die inhaling it after ten years." I told her to practice not letting others bother her and not letting herself ruminate so much about things that may not even happen. In other words, I encouraged her to not "leave any impressions or traces" that may affect her. So she tied a piece of red string around her finger. Every time she sees it, she reminds herself that "It's all good."

Is everything good? Of course not. But if impressions and traces remain in our minds, then even when things are good we make them out to not be good. Most of the time, we are just responding to the world through our own ideas and ideals. These are the impressions or traces. As practitioners, we need to learn to relate to others and take care of various affairs as if nothing has been done. How? By not injecting ourselves—our own benefit and harm, gain and loss, preferences of good and bad—into whatever we do. We must be careful to not project *our* values and *our* standards onto others. It doesn't mean we shouldn't have any standards. We need them. But if our standards create emotional afflictions, then that's a sure indicator that self-grasping is present.

One of the main reasons I left monasticism was because I felt buddhadharma must be brought beyond the walls of the monastery. I felt sheltered in the monastery. Even though I counseled practitioners about their vexations—which meant I was mostly dealing with their emotions—I had no idea what they were going through. I wanted to reenter the world and experience it so that I would know suffering. I had a conversation with my teacher about this. I said, "Shifu, how do we help people if we don't even know what they are feeling—how they are suffering?" He said, "You don't have to be sick to be a doctor. A doctor doesn't have to have cancer to cure it. The doctor just gives the medicine." But I said, "Shifu, if we don't know what they are sick with, how do we give out the right medicine?" Shifu said to me, "It's dangerous to jump into the ocean. There's no guarantee that you'll return." I was self-confident, and so I said, "I'll return!" Then, a year after I left, I asked him if I could come back. "The world is too hard!" I said. Shifu said, "No. I thought you wanted to save all beings. Finish your PhD, then we'll talk about it."

Difficult, difficult! It was so difficult in the beginning. I barely survived the world, and the only reason I did was because the bottom of this barrel had some holes in it already. If it hadn't, I would have drowned in the ocean of samsara. Now the pain or grief of the people I meet are like my pain and grief. At the same time, there is no pain or grief and there is no me. In offering this body and mind to others, there's no one to help and there is no helper. Yet, we seem to help ourselves with the teachings. Buddhadharma circulates of its own accord.

> Not being subjected [to form], you will embrace the myriad forms and appearances in the vastness of *dharmadhatu*. There will not be any outflows whatsoever.

Being "subjected" to form means you're affected by things. There is subject and object, refusal and acceptance. It's like the waves of an ocean. The ocean is not separated from or subjected to the waves. From the perspective of the waves, there are only waves. A wave, great or little, threatening or peaceful, is just a wave. It may go up, it may go down. When it is up, it is defined by its height; when it recedes, it is defined by how low it recedes. But whether it goes up or down, it is still part of the ocean. Be the ocean, not the waves.

This is what it means to "embrace the myriad forms and appearances in the vastness of *dharmadhatu.*"

Dharmadhatu can be understood as the world in this context. "Outflow" in Sanskrit is *ashrava*, literally "contaminated" or "flawed." Flawed how? What is it that flows out? Emotional afflictions. For many of us, afflictions are constantly leaking out of our senses, coloring and shaping the way we act, speak, and think. So this passage means, engage with the world but don't reify your experiences into *things*—self and others—and certainly don't generate afflictions.

How do we investigate Chan? Hongzhi is so kind, like a grandmother, presenting us with step-by-step guidelines for practice. Don't chase after awakening, and don't worry about not seeing your self-nature. Never try to get rid of the self that doesn't exist in the first place. Just work on afflictions and habit tendencies. Work on yourself. How? Sometimes you need to watch for pretentiousness. Other times you need to be still and shut up. Or you need to purify, be innocent, and genuine. Just expose, accept, and work with what you have. Don't contrive, don't reify things, don't solidify experiences, and don't create waves where there aren't any. Nothing's outside of you. Your true nature is vast like the ocean, able to embrace all. Just stop separating yourself from the world. If you keep placing everything outside of yourself, you end up feeling isolated. But if you get to a point in which you experience the unified state of oneness or awakening, put that down as well!

10. MULTITASKING

THE TEACHING in the following excerpt is about post-awakening practice in daily life. Life can be chaotic, and that's why it is a great training ground for integrating what we have learned and experienced. If we were to confine practice to the meditation cushion, then it would be quite useless. By engaging the world in a meaningful way, avail yourself of all the ups and downs and chaos. These will draw out our inner resources to work through all of our relationships. Then, we return to who we really are—buddhas.

> Multitasking amid chaos, manifesting in places of encounter—none of these are realms outside of yourself. Heaven and earth share the same root; the myriad forms are of a single body. Adapting to changes and transforming freely without being manipulated by those who curry favor—this is to actualize great freedom. Traveling like the wind; illuminating like the moon; encountering things without obstructions. Then and there, while resting and retreating, you shoulder the responsibility. When wisdom flows and the principle is perfected, practice will be forgotten but your role will be fulfilled—without you being trapped with the need for respect and honor. Entering the currents to be one with the dusty world, you transcend everything and shine in brilliance. Know that continuing in this fashion is genuine practice; but when there is discontinuity, there is no practice.

We live in what appears to be a world of confusion. Despite our attempts to bring order to life, things happen beyond our control, with misunderstandings between people and wrongheaded intentions. We bring our own baggage to our lives. Some want fame and recognition; others want money and power; still others just want to be left in peace. In our interactions, it is hard to have a meeting of minds and hearts. We live together, connected, but each of us is alone.

We use the technology of smartphones and social media to connect with others, but without intention, technology starts to dictate our lives. Our addiction to technology subjects us to a world of cyber dystopia.[1] In the end, we're still alone. With so much going on around us, fearing that we might be missing out, we are lost in all the ten thousand things we have to do. This is because we have no anchor, we are not grounded.

> Multitasking amid chaos, manifesting in places of encounter—
> none of these are realms outside of yourself.

Usually multitasking distracts us and fosters confusion. But here, multitasking is a metaphor for the wondrous function of selfless wisdom where tasks accomplish themselves, without effort or chaos. Multitasking is not something like a skill that you learn or force to happen. It is simply causes and conditions at work—with the self out of the way. There's nothing outside of us, nor is there any confusion—all that we encounter is within the interconnectedness of the present moment. When self-reference is present, however, there are only narrow perspectives and contrived effort. Things are out of our control, with no end in sight.

"Busyness" is an idea. In each moment, there is only what *can* be done, what *needs* to be done. When you can't finish a task, continue working on it tomorrow. If tomorrow it's still not done, then work on it the next day. Moment after moment, all things get done. But don't think *you* are accomplishing tasks; it's just causes and conditions interacting with causes and conditions. They have lasting impact on everything else, through time and space, beyond the purview of *your* ideas or intentions in this moment. When selfless wisdom functions, the effects of our actions bring about multiple benefits to all beings, past, present, and future. This is multitasking. It is not our ordinary idea of multitasking.

How do we truly connect with ourselves? How do we encounter others? In this world of chaos, we must begin by being in our bodies, connecting to our hearts. We must realize that nothing exists outside of ourselves, that there *is* no separate "other." If you experience an other, this very belief separates you from everything. When you bring this belief to your encounters, along with all your fixed ideas and projections, you end up feeling alienated and alone. When this happens, there is no encounter at all. If there is, it happens merely by chance, and it is so fleeting that soon you're back to aloneness.

So "none of these are realms outside of yourself" means everything is within you. Practice is about relationships, and we start with accepting ourselves. When we can do this intimately, we are able to connect with others—and things—as ourselves. Our heart is open and receptive. This is the way to have a true encounter.

In this connectedness, we don't reify experiences and notions into *things*. When we make a thing out of experiences, which are naturally fluid and open, we create walls and obstacles. Keep experiences fluid. Embrace everything. Amid thoughts and feelings, amid all our expectations and projections, we allow them to flow, to be. This is the teaching of the *Platform Scripture*: Internally no fixed thoughts; externally no fixed forms; mind arising, non-abiding. Inside, outside, are all ourselves, and this connection to everything is moment to moment, wakefully living in non-abiding. Don't allow the external world—the other—to dictate your experience. Allow this experiencing of intimacy and connectedness to bring meaning to everything.

To do this, first be aware of the underlying tones of your feelings. Cultivate the right attitudes of contentment, interest, confidence, and determination (see chapters 3 and 4). Then allow these to permeate the world and everything you do. This is not to say you project your own feelings onto the world—that would just be imagination. Instead, cultivating the right attitude of contentment allows you to be more open to what is happening. This is how "manifesting in places of encounter" works. What is manifesting? Non-abiding, emptiness. This means your natural selfless wisdom.

In Buddhism we make use of a wonderful Sanskrit word, *prapancha*. It means "conceptual proliferation." It refers to confusing imagination with reality. When you inject your own ideas (imagination) of how things are, you deny others their existence. This is *prapancha*. All things exist, but they don't exist in *your* ideas of how they exist. Others have their own ideas, their own perspectives, and they are trying to be happy. It may not be your sense of happiness, but they are trying. Give them a chance to be as they are.

Every moment is a new beginning. If you keep yourself out of the picture, then you begin to see fluidity, and there's a chance for real encounter. When you are receptive and open, you are able to experience all people and affairs as mirrors that respond to one another naturally. All things meet one another mind-to-mind, heart-to-heart. When there is no-self, you meet everything and everyone heart-to-heart. A single action accomplishes multiple tasks, and all are accomplished in their own accord. This is living wisdom, natural compassion—your birthright, awakening.

Earlier I mentioned the Chan saying "Watch what's right under your feet." It reminds us to pay attention to this moment, this step, even while walking up one hundred steps. If you keep dwelling on the number of steps—"Oh, my, there are so many steps! There's still so many more to go"—if your mind is dwelling in the future, then you might not move at all. Or everything slows down and the process takes a long time. Every step becomes a burden because the weight of the future is in the present. Instead, pay attention to *this* step. Right under your feet. One step, one step, one step. Before you know it, you've climbed up one hundred steps.

I've witnessed this in my teacher. We would travel great distances together to lead retreats. Soon after returning back to New York, he would have finished a book about the trip! He could see and absorb so much. Even though we had both been at the same place together, our experiences were very different, as if we had been at different places. I recall asking him, "Shifu, how did you do that?" He said, "I just write a little bit at a time. I squeeze in a little bit of time here and there. Today, one page. Tomorrow, another page. Sometimes when there is a long stretch of time I am able to write a lot."

Meanwhile he was taking care of building the Dharma Drum Mountain complex in Taiwan. As the buildings were being designed, he had to deal with different zoning codes, the application process, various stipulations. On top of that, he had to work with fools like me giving him a hard time. Most of the monastics were younger, in their twenties. I was the youngest. I was his attendant, but I'm ashamed to say that when we traveled here or there, many times he had to attend to me because of my absentminded-ness and immaturity! All the while, he took care of the construction, gave public talks to thousands of people, led hundreds of intensive retreats, and published numerous works. In each of those endeavors, multiple people benefitted. Multiple tasks were accomplished in a single act.

Being in the present moment doesn't mean just doing one simple task at a time. It may start that way, but as you practice, you will be able to accomplish a great deal so long as you accord with selfless wisdom. Each task you do will have multiple effects and infinite outcomes. If your self is out of the way, your wisdom and compassion will shine forth, in accord with causes and conditions, to help all beings around you without willing yourself to do so. Studying with my teacher, living with him, traveling with him, observing him, I learned that a busy person has the most amount of time. Only a lazy person is always out of time.

> Heaven and earth share the same root; the myriad forms are of a single body. Adapting to changes and transforming freely without being manipulated by those who curry favor—this is to actualize great freedom.

All things are created by the mind. The so-called mind is just a continual string of moment-to-moment thoughts. Some are coarse; others are subtle. Even when there appear to be no thoughts or particular feelings, there is a subtle undercurrent of tones of preconceptual feelings. These are also thoughts. The above line, "Heaven and earth share the same root; the myriad forms are of a single body," just means that our minds are the root of all experiences, and all forms are not outside of the four elements of earth, water, fire, and air. Whether these elements manifest as our bodies, or take the shape of the world outside, there really is no inside or outside.

In the West, people don't talk of heaven and earth—that's a Chinese expression for the whole world. Wasn't it William Blake who said that the whole world exists in a grain of sand? All things exist right here. Where is here? Is it there? Outside? Is it inside? Here just means you don't experience separateness.

The "myriad forms" refer to the changing conditions of the world. We need to recognize change when it occurs; we need to work with change as it happens. Sometimes we have to wait for change to happen. We can't force it. Other times we have to introduce change, or we have to change ourselves. This is the meaning of "adapting to changes and transforming freely." When we're receptive, non-abiding, we are not fixated on one way of doing things.

The Chinese word for what is rendered here as "those who curry favor" actually means "brownnosers"—those who do things in order to get ahead, people who want to manipulate things their way. You know what I'm talking about? For example, you see your boss and you have an intention to get on their good side so you say, "I like your new haircut. It looks great!" Meanwhile, what you really want to ask is, "Can I have next Monday and Tuesday off from work?" The significance of this line is that one should not be manipulated by people.

Some people think Buddhist practitioners are all "nice, compassionate people"—a euphemism for pushovers. They think we let everyone walk all over us. Nonsense! Just because we feel connected and we practice not experiencing things in a divisive way doesn't mean we don't know what's going on around us. We engage with the world, but we should not be manipulated into the games of the world. Children play games. It's what they do; they learn through playing games. In a game with a child, are you fooled by children? Some people may be, but generally, when a three- or five-year-old tries to pull a fast one on you, you should be able to see through it. Right? We expose, embrace, play along, and brush it off. There's no need to get upset. Sometimes we simply play along, but at a critical point, when the game becomes dangerous, or when people are getting hurt, you stop the game.

This analogy is not about infantilizing people or treating everyone as a child. That would be patronizing. The point is, when you learn to experience everything as not outside of yourself, there's an intimacy with all that you experience, all those you meet. When you cultivate this attitude of a wide and embracing heart, you can accept everyone. At the same time, you can choose to play the game in a way that's helpful. This means allowing people to genuinely be. This is practicing buddhadharma.

There's a time for everything. Sometimes we have to say no to a person, but later, when causes and conditions are suitable, we welcome that person into our lives again. The point is, we cultivate an attitude of embracing all without discriminations or obstructions. At the same time, we are able to adapt to changes and respond appropriately.

> Traveling like the wind; illuminating like the moon; encountering things without obstructions. Then and there, while resting and retreating, you shoulder the responsibility.

These words describe the selfless function of wisdom, responding to everything and everyone effortlessly and appropriately. Such wisdom is also called living compassion, where we are connected to ourselves and others, able to embrace everything and everyone. This is to encounter things without obstructions and self-referential attachments. But what about our responsibility?

Before awakening, responsibility is something we remind ourselves of, something we feel compelled to do. Whatever it may derive from—be it love, a sense of justice, or compassion for others—something is driving us to shoulder the responsibility. No matter how lofty the reason, there is always a self. When self is involved, there are always going to be difficulties and setbacks, and that's why we need to practice.

Chan practitioners cultivate the bodhi-mind, an altruistic responsibility to help everyone through a recognition that we are all connected. All that we have, all that we are, comes from others: the things we use, the food we eat, and everything we take for granted comes from others. What have we done to contribute to humanity? Are we only taking, without giving back? How can we forsake others and seek our own benefit? Reflecting on these truths, we feel humbled and grateful. This humility keeps our self-righteousness at bay; gratitude propels us to repay all that we have already received back to humanity, and indeed, all beings. To a bodhisattva practitioner, sentient beings are precious.

Bodhi means "awakening." Bodhi-mind means the mind that aspires for awakening, not only for ourselves but for everyone. That is, in order to be awakened, you must help others. It's not like you help others only *after* you're awakened. That kind of self-referential thinking will not do. It actually prevents you from awakening. For example, in Chan we chant what is known as the "Four Great Vows":

> I vow to save innumerable sentient beings
> I vow to cut off endless vexations
> I vow to master limitless approaches to dharma
> I vow to attain supreme buddhahood.

This formulation lays out the blueprint for practice. How do we become a buddha? We have to master limitless approaches to dharma. We have to practice. This doesn't necessarily mean we change methods all the time. Even with one method, adapting to different circumstances, there are infinite approaches to using it. Also, buddhadharma exists in life. So life, in all of its complexities, is practice. What is the point of practice? Putting an end to all our emotional afflictions. How do we end afflictions? We engage with all beings. In this process, we expose, embrace, work through, and let go of self-reference. The *Vimalakirti-sutra* says, "Sentient beings are in themselves the buddha land."[2] All buddhas have their own realm of awakening. You cannot become a buddha and have no buddha land of your own. The point of this line is, it is precisely due to sentient beings that one attains buddhahood. So it all comes down to sentient beings. They are the source of buddhahood— they are the cause of awakening.

In the cultivation of this selfless bodhisattva path, self-centeredness diminishes. In time, naturally, we accord with no-self. This is when awakening occurs. When you least expect it, self drops away. At that time, responding to the world is like the wind blowing or the moon illuminating—there is no contrivance, there are no obstructions. Helping others is like "resting and retreating." Is there a need to remind ourselves to be compassionate, or to speak of responsibility? No. Yet, our bodhisattva actions continue.

At that time, practice is natural and "forgotten":

> When wisdom flows and the principle is perfected, practice will be forgotten but your role will be fulfilled—without you being trapped with the need for respect and honor. Entering the currents to be one with the dusty world, you transcend everything and shine in brilliance.

With no contrivance, we continue the bodhisattva path, and all practices are completed. Completing everything, we will not feel proud, "Hey, look at all that I've done!" There's no need for reward or recognition, respect or honor.

Many people do good work, and this is wonderful, but sometimes the good work is tainted with vexations. All of our actions are in one way or another contaminated with vexations, such as a need for respect or honor. It is very hard not to seek recognition. I have an older dharma brother who devoted all of his life to helping others. He is mild-tempered and kind, with a gentle spirit. He practices chastity, frugality, and, of course, the bodhisattva path. However, there's one thing that he seem to always need: respect. You can't say he's not practicing, because he is. Nor can you say his good work is inadequate because he has helped many people. However, because of his need for reciprocity, respect, and honor, he cannot truly "transcend everything and shine in brilliance." Why? Because the self is present. We all have our shortcomings, and there are reasons why we are the way we are. It is up to each of us to do something about them. No one can do it for us.

> Know that continuing in this fashion is genuine practice; but when there is discontinuity, there is no practice.

The last line is really an encouragement to practice without giving up. The more we expose, embrace, and transform our shortcomings, the more we are able to let go of them and discover more. Only through practicing in life, mingling with all kinds of people, will we be able to deepen our Chan practice. Stopping is not an option. Even after awakening, we still need to work on subtle habit tendencies. Practice continues on and on.

PART THREE
Translations

THIS SECTION of the book is a running translation of twenty-five excerpts from fascicle or chapter 6 of master Hongzhi's discourse records, which can be found in the East Asian Taisho Buddhist canon, *Hongzhi chanshi guanglu* (The Extended Discourse Records of Chan Master Hongzhi), T. no. 2001, volume 48. The square brackets below, before each excerpt, refer to the page and column numbers in fascicle 6 of Hongzhi's work.

Hongzhi's discourse records are one of the longest for any single Chan master. He was a prolific writer. My earliest translation of some of the excerpts in this book dates back to the early 1990s. Since then, fascicle 6 of his work has been translated by Rev. Taigen Dan Leighton with the help of a Chinese literary scholar, Yi Wu, among others, in *Cultivating the Empty Field*. His translation provides an excellent flavor of Hongzhi's teachings. However, in my humble opinion, I hope that my own translation highlights further subtleties and nuances of Hongzhi's teaching. His reading also places Hongzhi's teaching squarely within the Japanese Soto Zen perspective of *shikantaza*, or "just sitting" practice. I see Hongzhi's teaching as belonging to a shared language of Chan. As I show in the introduction, many Chan masters—including those from other lineages—also articulated practice and awakening in similar language. While rendering Hongzhi's teaching through the lens of Soto Zen practice is useful, it also unintentionally reinforces sectarian divides and limits the broader significance of Hongzhi's message.

In the excerpts below I annotate some of the key ideas in the endnotes and provide the source of Hongzhi's quotes whenever he cites sayings by earlier masters. Many of these terms carry specific shades of meaning. You may read these excerpts straight through to get the flavor of Hongzi's teachings, or you can study them one by one with the aid of my annotations.

11. Hongzhi's Collected Writings on Silent Illumination

The Vacant Field

[73c05]

This vacant and open field is intrinsically present from the very beginning. You must purify and wipe away the various deluded conditioning and illusory habits. Naturally, you will arrive at a place that is clear and pure, perfect and bright. Totally empty, without any image; resplendent and outstanding, it does not rely on anything. Only this vastness can illuminate the fundamental reality as external objects are relinquished. Therefore, it is said, "With perfect clarity, there is not a single thing to be perceived."[1] This field is where birth and death do not reach. It is the source of utter luminosity, able to emit light and respond clearly to the myriad dust motes [of sensory objects]. It is empty, without oppositions. The wondrous [activity] of seeing and hearing leaps far beyond those everyday sounds and forms. In all situations, its functioning is without trace; its mirroring is without obstruction. Mind and its objects naturally and spontaneously issue forth without partiality. An ancient said, "Having no-mind, one attains in oneself the Way of no-mind. Actualizing no-mind in oneself, the Way ceases to be."[2] Advancing in such a way, you will be able to take up the responsibility [of helping sentient beings] with pure intent, as if you are sitting in perfect silence. As for the wondrous activity of leisurely entering the world, it is something you must investigate in this fashion!

Genuine Practice

[73c14]

Genuine practice is to simply sit in stillness and investigate this silence. In its profound depth, there is the realization where, externally, you can no longer be swayed by causes and conditions. Mind being empty, it is all-embracing; its luminosity being wondrous, it is precisely apt and impartial. Internally, there are no thoughts of grasping after things. Vast, solitary—the mind is [originally] free from dullness. Being alive and potent, you are able to sever all opposition and remain content.[3] Being content has nothing to do with emotions.[4] You must be open and spacious, relying on nothing whatsoever. Splendid and marvelous, [your mind] is full of life and spirit. Henceforth, it doesn't fall into defiling appearance. At peace under all circumstances, [mind] is pure and bright. Its luminosity is penetrating, able to respond smoothly in accordance with phenomena, where each and every phenomenon does not obstruct the other. Floating effortlessly, clouds appear on mountain peaks. Shining boldly, the moon is reflected in the mountain stream. Radiant luminosity and spiritual transformation manifest everywhere without the appearance of obstructions, mutually responding, like a container and its cover or shooting arrows meeting at the tip. With further training and nourishment, [your awakening] matures and is firmly embodied—clear under all situations. Cut off sharp corners; don't reason [about right and wrong]. Like a white ox or a tamed ferret that naturally responds to any command, you can be called a complete person. Therefore, it is said, "Having the way of no-mind, one can be like this; not having yet gained no-mind, it is extremely difficult!"[5]

SPIRITUAL POTENCY

[73C25]

[Mind], being wide and far-reaching, is without limit. Pure and clean, it emits light. Its spiritual potency[6] is unobscured and, because it is bright, no objects are illuminated.[7] It can be said to be empty,[8] yet this emptiness is [full of] luminosity. This luminosity is pure in and of itself, beyond causes and conditions and apart from subject and object. Its wondrousness is ever present, and the illumination is vast. Moreover, this is not something that can be conceived of as having the appearances of existence or nonexistence. Nor can it be spoken about with words and analogies. Right here, around this pivotal axis,[9] the gate swings effortlessly open and shut in response [to circumstances]. Such great functioning [of wisdom] is not inert. At all places, revolving and turning about, [this great functioning] does not follow conditions nor can it be trapped in models. In the midst of it all, it settles securely. With "that," it is identical to "that"; with "this," it is identical to "this." "This" and "that" merge without separation. Therefore, it is said, "Like the earth that holds up a mountain, unaware of its steepness and loftiness; like the stone that contains jade, unaware of its flawlessness. If you can be thus, this is truly leaving home."[10] Home leavers must embody the practice in this fashion.

WITHERING AWAY THOUGHTS

[74A05]

Patched-robe monks: wither away and freeze your [deluded] thinking; put to rest the remaining conditionings. Single-mindedly[11] wipe clean this field and directly hoe down all the overgrown grass. Throughout the four directions, there should not be a single speck of contaminating dust.[12] Spiritually potent and bright, vast and transparent, illuminate thoroughly and embody that which appears before you until the illumination becomes completely resplendent and no dust can be found. This is as easy as tugging and pulling back an ox[-mind] by the nose. Naturally, [this ox] will become noble and majestic. Being outstanding, it mingles with others along the path without damaging people's sprouts and grain. Moving along effortlessly, the ox does not need to be tethered, nor is it fixed in any location. This is how the ox tills through the field of the empty *kalpa*.[13] Proceeding in such a way, all things appear vividly without obscurity, and everything manifests as it is: one thought for ten thousand years.[14] Since the beginning, reality has always been non-abiding. Thus it is said, "The mind-ground contains the various seeds, which will sprout by the universal rain. Upon sudden awakening, the fruit of bodhi of its own accord."[15]

YOUR HOME

[74A14]

It cannot be practiced nor actualized because it is intrinsically complete. Others cannot tarnish it; it is thoroughly immaculate to its depth. Precisely at the place of immaculacy, fix your gaze upon it and thoroughly illuminate and relinquish everything. Experiencing this clarity, grounding yourself firmly, [you will see that] birth and death originally have no root or stem, and emerging and sinking are fundamentally without trace.[16] When your intrinsic splendor reaches its peak, it is empty yet potent. When your original wisdom responds to conditions, it is quiescent but resplendent. Genuinely arriving at this place where there is no middle or extremes, before or after, your practice begins to be one pervasive whole. On each and every occasion, the interaction of your sense faculties and objects is itself the preaching of buddhadharma[17] transmitting the inexhaustible lamp. Everything emits great radiance, everything is performing the great work of accomplishing buddhahood. Originally, you do not need a hair's breadth of an external object. Clearly, this is a matter to be found within your own home.

MULTITASKING

[74A22]

Multitasking amid chaos, manifesting in places of encounter—none of these are realms outside of yourself. Heaven and earth share the same root; the myriad forms are of a single body. Adapting to changes and transforming freely without being manipulated by those who curry favor—this is to actualize great freedom. Traveling like the wind; illuminating like the moon; encountering things without obstructions. Then and there, while resting and retreating, you shoulder the responsibility. When wisdom flows and the principle is perfected, practice will be forgotten but your role will be fulfilled—without you being trapped with the need for respect and honor. Entering the currents to be one with the dusty world, you transcend everything and shine in brilliance. Know that continuing in this fashion is genuine practice; but when there is discontinuity, there is no practice.

THE FAMILY AFFAIR

[74A28]

Peel away your scalp and allow the light to shine forth. There is a place where the myriad calculations and schemes do not reach and a [truth that even a] thousand sages cannot transmit. This is something that only you can illuminate and profoundly verify. Accord with it intimately and your intrinsic luminosity will dispel all darkness. Genuine luminosity reflects far beyond measure, transcending both existence and nonexistence. Wonder exists in experiencing whatever manifests before you. Accomplishment is outside of this present *kalpa*. Adapt to conditions and merge with awakening; then you will not be obstructed by the myriad dust motes. Moment to moment, mind does not encounter *things*; step-by-step, no traces are left on the path. This is called being able to carry on the family affair [of the buddhas]. To be thoroughly penetrating like this is something you have to become intimate with.

THE INVESTIGATION

[74B05]

Being unpretentious and empty, pure and still, cold and dispassionate, innocent and genuine—this is how to eradicate countless lifetimes of accumulated habit tendencies. The moment habit tendencies and defilements exhaust themselves, intrinsic luminosity will manifest, blazing through your skull. Vacant of external things, cleansed and spacious—like the merging of the sky and the autumn lake. Like the sameness of the snow against the winter moon. This field has no horizons or boundaries—it cannot be measured. When it is experienced as one vast expansive continuity without any sharp corners or seams, you must thoroughly relinquish this [experience]. This relinquishing is not something that can be conceived of or theorized about through discursive reasoning. How can it be gained through instructions or comments? Only one whose bottom of the barrel has fallen off can be convinced of this. Thus it is said, "Only by actualizing it would one be in accordance with it."[18] To be in accordance with it is to enter the world to roam and play in samadhi, where everything manifests as it is. Sounds and forms, shadows and echoes are engaged with directly, yet none of them leave any impressions or traces. In the midst of it all, it is as if there have never been interactions or responses. Not being subjected [to form], you will embrace the myriad forms and appearances in the vastness of *dharmadhatu*. There will not be any outflows whatsoever. Person of true color, investigate this in this fashion.

THE WHITE OX

[74B16]

What patched-robe monks cultivate is the ability to thoroughly let go—to not get caught up with even a single hair's breadth [of attachment]. Wide and open, translucent and pure, like a mirror reflecting mirrors—there are no external objects or separate conditions. Self-illuminating and experiencing like this, you will not be subjected to anything. This is called taking up the responsibility right away. When you take up the responsibility like this, your wisdom is able to illuminate the obscure without torpor, and you embody the way without abidance. From non-abiding, respond and change appropriately with great precision, but without outflows or contaminants. Like the valley spirit responding to sounds or the wind master soaring through the sky, you will be self-at-ease without any hindrance at all. Don't try to control or extinguish traces [of your mind]. Yet be wakeful and alert—never unclear. Roaming freely in the fields with perfection, you will be able to firmly and leisurely settle everywhere. This white ox, exposed out in the open,[19] immaculate and pure, cannot be taken advantage of. You must personally actualize and arrive at this state.

OPEN THE GRASPING HANDS

[74B25]

Silent and still, abiding in itself, this suchness is apart from conditioning. Its luminosity is vast and spacious, without any dust. Directly, [delusion] is thoroughly relinquished. Arriving at this fundamental place, you realize that it is not something newly acquired today. Since before the ancient abode of the great *kalpa*,[20] there has always been the presence of utter clarity without any obscurations. Potent and lively, it shines alone. Though it is like this, it must be actualized. To actualize it in this moment is simply to not allow a single thing to arise, a single speck of dust to cover it. In this great rest, [let all conditioning] dry up and freeze, and be spacious and completely lucid. If this great rest is not thoroughly exhaustive, you will not be able to reach the realm beyond birth and death. Directly penetrate through and don't engage in dustlike intentions; dissolve your concern. Just take a backward step and open your grasping hands. Thoroughly resolve this matter. Only then will you be able to put forth light and respond to the world appropriately, merging with the myriad objects in a manner that is just right for all occasions. It is said, "The truth of all dharmas is not hidden; from ancient times to the present, it is always revealing itself."[21]

TURNING INWARD

[74C05]

The genuineness of patched-robe monks lies in their actualization of practice. Thoroughly illuminate the subtleties of the source, which is featureless yet radiant, of a single color and without any marks. You must turn inward in order to realize it. This is called taking care of the family affairs. Without a single thread of attachment, dissolve away both light and shadows—this is your forefathers' path, the wonder of which can only be personally experienced. It is where all dust and dregs have vanished, where knots are disentangled. Merely understanding it does not compare to reverting your ways and verifying it for yourself. Perceive right through this skeletal cadaver and right in the midst of it, realize [awakening]. Only then will you be able to manifest [this source]. Like the flowering reeds blowing under the bright autumn moon; like the ancient ferryboat drifting off into the sea; like the jade threads that loop through the golden embroidery needle—these are the occasions to return and enter the world in response to the multitude of conditions. All things are just you—there is no "other." Sailing along, following the wind—you are natural and free from impediments.

How to Proceed

[74c13]

All the buddhas and ancestral masters do not actualize anything different—they all arrive at this resting place where the three times [of past, present, and future] are severed, and the myriad conditions are silenced. Directly there is not a single hair's breadth of opposition. The spirited buddha illuminates spontaneously, and this sublime illumination thoroughly penetrates to the source. When your realization is far-reaching and exhaustive, you multiply in response to the multitude of circumstances.[22] As illumination issues forth through your sense doors, the sensory objects appear like cast shadows. You will then realize that all things flow out from yourself. The hundreds of thousands of situations[23] are no longer the causes or conditions that oppose you. Thorough and penetrating right through your whole being—this is how to proceed!

Dissolving the Self

[74c18]

Being empty, it leaves no traces; in illumination there are no dustlike emotions. When the light penetrates, the stillness is profound; mysteriously it severs all defects. When you perceive the self in this fashion, you dissolve this self at once. This field is clear and pure, wondrous and bright—it is that which is intrinsic within you. Many lifetimes of inability to resolve [this matter] come only from obscuring doubts and concealing delusions. All these are but self-created hindrances and blocks. Openly allow your wisdom to roam freely; internally, forget about merit and reward. Just directly relinquish this burden. Turn around and resume your position. Put your feet firmly on the way. In spontaneous responsiveness and wondrous functioning, all things encountered are reality. Here, there is not a single thing— from the tiniest hair to a speck of dust—outside yourself.

CONTINUOUS REALIZATION
[74C24]

Each and every dharma is spontaneously natural—wonder is beyond words and descriptions. When your realization becomes continuous, all the mountain forests and grasslands demonstrate this affair [of awakening]. If you're able to perceive right through delusion, you will realize that nothing is concealing buddha's broad, long tongue [expounding the dharma]. The expounding is itself listening; the listening is itself expounding. Sense faculties and objects merge as principle and wisdom fuse together. When self and others are identified, mind and dharmas are one. Precisely discern this identity. Even though it is like this and you're able to penetrate that which appears before you, you must quickly retreat and work at this within your own house, so that it becomes stable.

ORIGINAL DWELLING PLACE
[75A16]

To contemplate the true form of the self is to contemplate buddha. If you can experience the realm where nothing exists outside of your [mind], then all opposites will be thoroughly extinguished, and all conceptions transcended. Buddha and mind are refined to their non-dual [nature]. This is where patched-robe monks silently roam, abiding in quiescence. Vacant yet potent, marvelous and permeating, their mind is comparable to the great space that surpasses this dustlike *kalpa*. Brilliant and profound, it is where all addictions cease. Luminous and bright, [mind] is without deliberations. This is your original dwelling place. When opportunity shifts,[24] [this illumination] transforms and emanates; passing through the world, it responds to all situations. This illumination is effortless; its function leaves no trace. Clouds leisurely drifting, streams naturally flowing—there have never been any lingering hindrances since the very beginning. Just be directly innocent and secure, then all is unmoving and no manipulating conditions can move you.[25] You must genuinely embody this.

TIMELESS ANCIENT ABODE

[75A23]

Descendants come from an ancestor; all streams have an origin. If you can thoroughly perceive the origin and the ancestor, then you will know that which exists before the proliferation of streams. Sitting in stillness, you won't flow with the accumulating conditions of birth and extinction. Even though you won't follow them, all affairs will exist like reflections and shadows. Awakened, the sense faculties and objects are transcended with full clarity. Understanding and perception are no longer contained by anything. Passions emptied, deliberations severed, you will naturally perfect this luminosity. Don't be confused amid the myriad floating reflections. Yet, within each mote of dust are boundless possibilities. The hundreds and thousands of samadhis, each lofty and majestic, are fulfilled within each situation. This is something you will have to master and bring home to this timeless, ancient abode. Revive this wellspring and honor your ancestor. Merge with appearances. Go on to perceive and embody everything!

THE PIVOTAL AXIS

[75B02]

Illumination in silence is likened to the clear autumn sky where this illumination is without effort,[26] and where [the duality of] light and shadow are severed—this is the moment when even genuine realization is transcended. When the source is pure, the experience of it becomes efficacious. When the pivotal axis is open, its mobility becomes lively. Clear and brilliant, it is intrinsically radiant. When this center is discovered, you will bring forth [its efficacy] and utilize it in manifold situations with full appropriateness. This is the identity of heaven and earth, where the ten thousand appearances are harmonized. Contented and poised, [you are] self-possessed and able to roam about freely in any direction.[27] Responding to heavenly beings in a heavenly appearance, delivering human beings in a human form, whatever the situation calls for you manifest the appropriate body and appearance to expound the dharma. If you can perfectly embody this in such a way, you will be vast and open, putting an end to all obstacles.

SIMPLICITY AND NATURALNESS

[75B08]

The tiger moves swiftly like the wind, and the dragon roams among the clouds. Each befittingly adapts to its environment. This adaptability is intrinsic to their nature and does not involve contrivance; it's all very natural. Similarly, the patched-robe monk's adaptability and clear perception harmonize with causes and conditions. Coming, they are unassuming; going, they don't hide themselves. Wondrously entering all places without being bewildered and rising above the ten thousand appearances, they brilliantly reside among the myriad forms. Without a hairbreadth gap, they merge with all and respond to opportunities—every response hits home. This is something that you must investigate fully. When the clouds vanish, the winds stop; as the autumn clears, the moon sets. The ocean and the sky are both limitless. In simplicity, brilliance is realized.

THE IMPERIAL EDICT

[75B15]

The truth is not [something] transmittable by ancestral masters.[28] Before their arrival, the imperial edict had already been issued throughout the whole world.[29] Naturally empty without any trace, [your true nature] is potent and spiritual; dualities cease. Solitary and luminous, it transcends causes and conditions. Eternally alive, it is not barren.[30] This is why [practice is] called becoming an ancestor. It can only be realized through mutual authentication; the ancestors cannot hand it to you. All buddhas arrive here and take this to be the ultimate, utilizing it to respond, transform, and disseminate their [emanation] bodies which are likened to [a multitude of] flowers and leaves.[31] Sense faculties and objects are but wisdom entering the three times [of past, present, and future]. The ten thousand opportunities do not disturb you; not a single dust mote is outside yourself. Its wonder is beyond the countless thousands of scriptures. How could the affairs that are like reflections and shadows be grasped?

THE LUCID LAKE

[75B21]

This lake is lucid and deep, tranquil and still. Its transparency penetrates thoroughly to the very bottom. It is vacant yet divine, spacious and resplendent. Even though the lake is able to reflect images, in it there are no images or affects. If in a moment you can experience a glimpse of it and pierce right through [to the bottom], then, even though there is merit for taking up the burden [of this great matter] to discern it clearly, it is all the more necessary that you take a backward step[32] and retreat to the center.[33] Illuminate right to the core. Even though it seems amazing and outstanding, solitary and immutable, you still need to relinquish such merit [of seeing your self-nature]. Only then is this called being "reborn."[34] Such is the obscurity and subtlety of emerging and sinking away [of sentient beings].[35] You must carefully discern the subtlety of realizations. Then, you can emanate different bodies and steer various affairs.

The Seal

[75B26]

The seal of ten thousand forms is a seal that leaves no imprints. Roaming the world, responding to conditions, you enjoy the function of being able to enter dust motes upon dust motes of samadhis. Such function is for your own use, and does not have limits. The empty valley receives clouds; the cold stream cleanses the moon. Not departing and not remaining, you will transcend ordinary circumstances and expound the teaching without gaining and responding. You are present everywhere, yet always remaining in the same field without moving a single hair's breadth. [You may be] crippled and needing assistance, or ugly and foolish, but you will naturally thrive in perfect accordance. Zhaozhou's responses, "Go wash your bowl"[36] and "Go drink tea"[37] are not premeditated acts. From the very beginning [awakening] is already complete.[38] When your insight can be like this, from one instant to the next, thorough and complete, your conduct can then be considered that of a patched-robe monk.

The Empty *Kalpa*

[76A20]

Where the field is secure and concealed, when activities are like a frozen pond, the empty *kalpa* is perceived. [In such a state,] there is not a single hair's breadth of condition that can become a burden; no single [dust] mote that can become an obstacle. Utterly empty, it is bright. Perfectly pure, it is resplendent. Existing in utter clarity, [the mind] extends throughout ten thousand eras without ever being hazy. With regard to this matter,[39] if you can be convinced with a nod of your head, you will neither conform to birth and death nor will you abide in nihilism or permanence. In motion, you transform along with the myriad [sentient beings]. In stillness, you are enduring like the way heaven covers and the way earth supports. Emerging and sinking away, rolling and unrolling,[40] everything is up to you. Fellows of true color, you must learn to bring it forth and let it go like this.

LEAVING NO TRACE

[77B04]

In utter clarity, wonder exists. Potent and solitary, it illumines. Grasped, it cannot be obtained, so it cannot be called existence; polished, it cannot be removed, so it cannot be called nonexistence. It is utterly beyond the domain of the conceptual mind and it is separated from any traces of shadows and appearances—wondrous, it is empty of its own being. This miraculous place can be experienced as spiritual potency; when potency is reached, it reverts back [to stillness]. Mind like moon, body like clouds, it is disclosed according to wherever one may be. Straightforwardly, it leaves no trace. Yet, it is able to issue forth light and luminosity.[41] Responding to objects without refusal, one enters the dusty [world] and is not mired. Breaking through all obstructing states and shining through all phenomena, it is devoid of selfhood. Why can it, through diverse conditions, enter the pure [realm of] wisdom and roam and play in samadhi? You should thus genuinely experience and investigate it!

ALREADY COMPLETE

[78A05]

Vast, it is intrinsically potent. Pure, it is bright in and of itself. It is universal and yet it does not grasp the merit of its own illumination. It is able to discern without being burdened by conditioned thinking. It appears without form. It transcends thoughts, imagination, and feelings. You can only be in accordance with it through actualization—it is not something obtained from someone else. All buddhas and ancestral masters, which are likened to [a multitude of] leaves and flowers, continue this affair. Responding, it does not grasp appearances; illuminating, it is not ensnared by conditions. Dignified and impressive, nothing is concealed in it. This is our family style;[42]

everywhere all things are already self-evident and complete of their own accord.[43] It is up to you to take charge of it.

THE WORDLESS TEACHING

[78B16]

Mind is intrinsically beyond conditioning; fundamentally, buddhadharma cannot be articulated. The buddhas and ancestral masters have not obtained anything. But at the second-tier level [of buddhadharma], there are admonitions of occasional questions and answers during which [such expedient means] could weed out and set aside those of sharp faculties from the dullards. For this reason, Deshan said, "Our school has no words and phrases; nor does it have anything to give to people."[44] It is only because people come and are willing to [seek advice] that there are words to be said that directly wash away deluded thinking and dirt. When dirt is purified, mind becomes vast and empty, lustrous and bright—with no horizon or borders, no middle or extremes. Perfectly intermingling, luminous and clear, you are able to thoroughly penetrate the ten directions and sit through the three periods of time.[45] Here, all the conditioning of words and language, like dust motes, cannot be grasped. Silently self-cognizant; potently luminous. Undifferentiated from the saintly and not diminished in the ordinary, it is the original state of affairs within our ancient abode. Since when does it have anything to do with seeking outside yourself? This is what is considered the genuine field. Those who can verify this for themselves are able to respond to the myriad situations and naturally enter into the multitude of realms with wondrous responsiveness and potent penetration without any obstructions.

Notes

Chapter 1: A Parable for Silent Illumination

1. This parable comes from the *Daban niepan jing* 大般涅槃經 (*Mahaparinirvana-sutra*); see T. no. 374, 12: 556a09–a21.

2. See *Hongzhi chanshi guanglu* 宏智禪師廣錄 (The Extended Discourse Record of Chan Master Hongzhi), T. no. 2001, 48: 74a14–16.

3. See *Hongzhi chanshi guanglu*, T. no. 2001, 48: 73c14–15.

4. See *Yuanwu Foguo chanshi yulu* 圓悟佛果禪師語錄 (The Discourse Record of Chan Master Yuanwu Foguo [Keqin]), T. no. 1997, 47: 787b21–22.

5. See *Dahui Pujue [Zong'gao] chanshi fayu* 大慧普覺禪師法語 (The Discourse Record of Chan Master Dahui Pujue [Zong'gao]), T. no. 1998a, 48: 891b5–9.

6. See *Hongzhi chanshi guanglu*, T. no. 2001, 48: 73c05–7.

7. Yongjia Xuanjue 永嘉玄覺 (665–713) was one of the first Chan masters who articulated silent illumination in terms of quiescence and wakefulness. For the passage above, see *Chanzong Yongjia ji* 禪宗永嘉集 (Collection of Yongjia of the Chan School), T. no. 2013, 48: 389b29–c1.

8. The quiescent and luminous mind here is a rendering for *jizhao* 寂照. Zhiyi 智顗 (539–598) of the Tiantai School here is describing the inconceivability of a single awareness, in perfect accordance with the "perfect teaching" (*yuanjiao* 圓教). For this passage, see *Miaofa lianhua jing xuanyi* 妙法蓮華經玄義 (The Sublime Meaning of the Wondrous Law of the Lotus Sutra), T. no. 1716, 33: 733a18–20.

9. Ibid., T. no. 1716, 33: 783b19 and 793a2.

10. See Fazang's 法藏 (643–712) *Huayan jing tanxuan ji* 華嚴經探玄記 (Record of the Search for the Profundities of the Huayan Sutra), T. no. 1733, 35: 214b17; or Chengguan's 澄觀 (738–839) *Da fangguang fo huayan jing shu* 大方廣佛華嚴經疏 (Commentary on the Flower Ornament Sutra), T. no. 1735, 35: 532a20. In both cases, the key word is also *jizhao* 寂照 or "quiescent luminosity." Chengguan uses this word extensively to describe not only the awakened state but also the ability to save all sentient beings. The above citation is just one example. If one uses the keyword *jizhao* to search his commentary, one will find dozens of instances.

CHAPTER 2: STARTING FROM WHERE WE ARE

1. For *Angulimala-sutta*, see *Majjhima Nikaya*, 86. The text is also available on the internet. For example, see: www.accesstoinsight.org/tipitaka/mn/mn.086.than.html.

CHAPTER 3: THE UNDERLYING FEELING TONES

1. For more on mental factors, see Guo Gu, "Integrating Yogacara in Your Practice," *Buddhadharma: The Practitioner's Quarterly* (Spring 2018): 77–88.
2. See *Hongzhi chanshi guanglu*, T. no. 2001, 48: 74b25–c02. A full translation of this passage appears in part 3 of this book.
3. See *Liuzu dashi fabao tanjing* 六祖大師法寶壇經 (The Platform Scripture of the Great Sixth Ancestral Master), T. no. 2008, 48: 353a11–a13. Hereafter, the *Platform Scripture*. For an alternative English translation of this passage, see John McRae, *The Platform Sutra of the Sixth Patriarch* (Numata Center for Buddhist Translation and Research, 2000), 43.
4. See *Liuzu dashi fabao tanjing*, T. no. 2008, 48: 353b20–b21; see McRae, *The Platform Sutra of the Sixth Patriarch*, 46.

CHAPTER 4: SUPPORTING ATTITUDES TO CULTIVATE

1. See *Dazhidu lun* 大智度論 (*Mahaprajnaparamita-shastra*), T no. 1509, 25: 63a01–2; see also *Du Huayan lueshu kanding ji* 續華嚴略疏刊定記 (Amended Record of Abbreviated Comments on Reading the *Avatamsaka-sutra*) by Huiyuan 慧苑 (673–743), X. no. 2221, 3: 652c22–23.

CHAPTER 5: MEDITATION

1. Neuroscientists confirm that "neurons that fire together, wire together." See Daniel J. Siegel, MD, *Mindsight: Change your Brain and Your Life* (Bantam, 2010), 290, n148.

CHAPTER 6: APPROACHES TO SILENT ILLUMINATION

1. See Guo Gu, "You Are Already Enlightened," *Buddhadharma: The Practitioner's Quarterly* (Winter 2012): 38–43.
2. See Yongjia Xuanjue, *Chanzong Yongjia ji* (Record of Yongjia in the Chan Tradition), T. no. 2013, 48: 389c1–2.
3. See R. Firth, "Sense-Data and Percept Theory," in *Perceiving, Sensing and Knowing*, ed. R. Swartz (Berkeley: University of California Press, 1965), 204–70.
4. For those who would like to explore this further, these are similar to the four kinds of karma in *Yogacharabhumi-shastra*'s: (1) the activity of cognizing the natural world (*liaobie qijie* 了別器業); (2) the activity of cognizing bases (*liaobie yiye*

了別依業); (3) the activity of cognizing a self (*liaobie wiye* 了別我業); and (4) the activity of cognizing objects (*liaobie jingye* 了別境業). See Yuqie shi dilun 瑜伽師 地論 (*Yogacharabhumi-shastra*), T. no. 1579, 30: 579c3.

5. How bare mental perception arises is one of the most obscure and debated aspects of Buddhist epistemology and is too large a subject to explain in detail here. There are different positions within the Yogachara tradition. I'm following the Chinese system of Kuiji 窺基 (632–682), who follows that of Dharmapala (mid-sixth century), himself a student of Dignaga 陣那. These two masters proposed that mental perceptions arise simultaneously with the five sensory perceptions and take the same object as the five sensory perceptions. This is the classic Yogachara view. For Dharmapala, see *Cheng weishi lun* 成唯識論, T. no. 1585, 31:21a; for Kuiji's commentary on this, see *Cheng weishi lun shuji* 成唯識論述記, T. no. 1830, 43: 389a, 420c. Dharmakirti (ca. sixth or seventh century), on the other hand, proposes that bare mental perception arises after sensory perceptions and takes a different object than that of sensory perceptions. This is actually a position held by early Sautrantika Hinayana Buddhists. Because Dharmakirti's view is contradictory with regard to the question of whether sense perceptions are self-cognizant or not, he provides conflicting answers to the question of the object. Sometimes he follows the Yogachara position, but other times he follows the Sautrantika view. As I'm speaking from the position of Chinese Buddhism, I follow the Chinese Yogachara view. The Tibetans teach mental perception following the Sautrantika view at the first level of the four doctrines they must master. They later refute it at the higher levels. For a discussion of whether mental perception is self-cognizant or not, see Zhihua Yao, *The Buddhist Theory of Self-Cognition* (London and New York: Routledge, 2005), 140–41.

6. Again, there are conflicting views on what is bare mental perception. Here, I am following the explanation of Kuiji on the simultaneous arising of mental perception and sensory perception. For an alternative Tibetan interpretation, see the teachings of Geshe Rabten, *The Mind and Its Functions* (Tharpa Choeling, 1979), 13.

7. For example, according to Dharmakirti, consciousness is aware of itself in a conceptual but non-dual way that does not involve the presence of a separate awareness of consciousness; see Dreyfus, *Recognizing Reality: Dharmakirti's Philosophy and Its Tibetan Interpretations* (Albany: SUNY, 1997), 339–40.

8. See Geshe Ngawang Dhargyey, *A Compendium of Ways of Knowing: A Clear Mirror of What Should Be Accepted and Rejected* (Dharamsala: Library of Tibetan Works and Archives, 1976), 26; Dreyfus, *Recognizing Reality*, 366.

9. Awakened being here refers to a "holy being." In Yogachara technical usage, a practitioner who is at the level of the path of insight or above. This person has not only seen self-nature but is deeply awakened according to the five paths of preparation, accumulation, insight, cultivation, and attainment. In addition to buddhas and bodhisattvas, the term "holy being" can also refer to arhats, *pratyekabuddhas*, and other kinds of beings on the path who are beyond the level of having anything to learn (*wuxue* 無學).

10. For this passage in the *Shurangama-sutra*, see *Da foding rulai miyin xiuzheng liaoyi zhupusa wanxing shoulengyan jing* 大佛頂如來密因修證了義諸菩薩萬行首楞嚴經, T. no. 945, 19: 128b18–19.

11. For the five points of stilling the mind, see Sheng-yen, *Hoofprints of the Ox* (Oxford: Oxford University Press, 2001), 65–91.

12. See *Liuzu dashi fabao tanjing*, T. no. 2008, 48: 352c14–16.

CHAPTER 7: CAVEATS AND PITFALLS

1. Ibid., T. no. 2008, 48: 353a02–5. For an alternative English translation of this passage, see McRae, *The Platform Sutra of the Sixth Patriarch*, 43. For the passage in the *Vimalakirti-sutra*, see T. no. 475, 14: 539c17–27. There are several English translations of this text. One good translation is by Burton Watson, *The Vimalakīrti Sūtra* (New York: Columbia University Press, 1997). The passage where Vimalakirti bodhisattva berates Shariputra can be found in chapter 3.

2. See *Liuzu dashi fabao tanjing*, T. no. 2008, 48: 353b08–12. For an alternative English rendering of this passage, see McRae, *The Platform Sutra of the Sixth Patriarch*, 45.

CHAPTER 8: THE VACANT FIELD

1. See Watson, *The Vimalakirti Sutra*, 83.

2. This passage is attributed to Chan master Banshan Baoji 盤山寶積 (eighth century), a dharma heir of great Chan master Mazu Daoyi 馬祖道一 (709–788); see *Jingde chuangdeng lu* 景德傳燈錄 (Transmission of the Flame in the Jingde Era), T. no. 2076, 51: 253b20–21.

CHAPTER 10: MULTITASKING

1. See Guo Gu, "Dharma Practice in an Age of Technological Dystopia," *Chan Magazine* 38, no. 1, 24–31.

2. See chapter 1 in the *Vimalakirti-sutra*. In Burton Watson's translation, the line in question is on p. 26.

CHAPTER 11: HONGZHI'S COLLECTED WRITINGS ON SILENT ILLUMINATION

1. "Not a single thing": Awakening is not a *thing* to be attained or realized. This can be said to be the fundamental position of Chan. It appears early on in the work attributed to Bodhidharma and continues to be repeated throughout the generations by all Chan masters. The earliest source for this idea is found in *Damo dashi xuemai lun* 達磨大師血脈論 (Treatise on the Blood and Marrow of Great Master Bodhidharma), 10, no. 1218, 63: 2c05. It is also repeated in the *Platform Scripture* or *Liuzu dashi fabao tanjing*, T. no. 2008, 48: 349a08, as well as Chan master

Huangpo's discourse record; see *Huangpo shan Duanji chanshi chuangxin fayao* 黃檗山斷際禪師傳心法要 (Essential Dharma of Transmitting the Mind by Chan Master Duanji of Mount Huangpo), T. 48, no. 2012A, 383c14, and *Huangpo Duanji chanshi wanling lu* 黃檗斷際禪師宛陵錄 (The Wanling Records of Chan Master Huangpo Duanji), T. no. 2012B, 48:387a06.

2. This quote is attributed to Longya Judun 龍牙居遁 (835–923); see *Chanmen zhuzushi jisong* 禪門諸祖師偈頌, X 66, no. 1298:726c16. However, the notion that "no mind is the way" dates to a much earlier time to the teaching of Sikong Benjing 司空本淨 (667–761), a disciple of Huineng the sixth ancestral master; see *Wudeng Huiyuan* 五燈會元 (Five Lamps Merging at the Source) 10, 80, no. 1565, 59b10–11.

3. What is rendered here as "content" is *zide* 自得, which implies self-sufficiency—needing nothing from outside of oneself—or self at ease.

4. What is rendered here as "emotions" is *qing* 情. In the premodern Confucian context, Chinese Buddhists understood *qing* as something negative, in opposition to *li* 理, which means "principle" or "reason." Thus, Chinese Buddhists often associate *qing* with the Sanskrit word *kleshas*, "emotional afflictions" or "vexations." At times, *qing* is also commonly coupled with the Chinese word *chen* 塵, which means "dust"; together, the word *qingchen* defines, in a derogatory way, the Buddhist notion of the six sense dusts or objects. This suggests that emotional afflictions arise from involvement with the six sense objects of sight, sound, taste, smell, touch, and thought. So, this line means that intrinsic luminosity is not something derived from the six sense objects. Luminosity is an inherent part of the nature of mind.

5. Hongzhi is paraphrasing Sikong Benjing; see note 2 above.

6. Spiritual potency is a rendering for the Chinese character *ling* 靈, which can also mean "lively," "agile," "dynamic," "spirited."

7. In awakening luminosity, there is no subject and object. Experiences are not reified into *things* to be grasped. Yet, all endeavors are accomplished. See my comments on subjectivity and subjecthood in chapter 2.

8. Here, "empty" is a rendering for the Chinese character *xu* 虛, which can also mean "vacant," "embracing," or "humility."

9. "Pivotal axis" is a rendering for the Chinese characters *shuji* 樞機, which in ancient China, refers to the central axis or part of a mechanism that makes everything turn, such as the axis of a loom. Here, it expresses the function of illumination, or wisdom.

10. See note 33 below.

11. "Single-mindedly" is a rendering for *yiwei* 一味, which literally means "with a single taste."

12. "Dust" here is a rendering for *chen* 塵, a Chinese term depicting the six sense objects. See note 38 below.

13. Empty *kalpa* or eon is a time during which buddhas do not appear in the world. Thus, this sentence may mean when the Buddha has passed away.

14. "One thought for ten thousand years" (*yinian wannian* 一念萬年) is a line from

"Faith in Mind" (*Xinxin ming* 信心銘), a work attributed to the third Chan ancestral master, Sengcan 僧璨 (d. 606); see T. no. 2010, 48: 377a04. It is an expression of timelessness. "One thought" can mean no-thought, the true reality of selflessness. For this reason, it is also referred to as "non-abiding." It can also mean meditative absorption.

15. This is a line from the last chapter of the *Platform Scripture*, T. no. 2008, 48: 361b08–9.

16. What is rendered here as "emerging and sinking" refers to birth and death; an allusion is made to the ocean of suffering where sentient beings are said to emerge and sink back into the ocean without end.

17. The literal translation of "preaching the buddhadharma" is "expounding with the broad and long tongue." The broad and long tongue is one of the thirty-two marks of a buddha. It symbolizes eloquence in expounding the dharma.

18. This expression appears in several of Chengguan's commentaries on the *Avatamsaka-sutra*; see, for example, *Fangguang fo huayan jing suishu yanyi chao* 方廣佛華嚴經隨疏演義鈔 (Commentary on the Vaipulya Huayan jing), T. no. 1736, 36: 123a15–16.

19. "The white ox exposed out in the open" (*ludi bainiu* 露地白牛) alludes to the *Lotus Sutra*, the chapter on the burning house where the Buddha used a parable of a merchant father who used three types of toy carts to lure his children out of the house. Once the children came out of the house, the father and the children "sat in the open ground" (*ludi erzuo* 露地而坐), and he presented them with a great white ox (*bainiu* 白牛) cart instead of "toy carts." The three toy carts represent the various expedient means of the *shravaka* (voice-hearer arhats), *pratyekabuddha* (solitary-awakened arhats), and bodhisattva vehicles. The great white ox represents the Buddha vehicle. The earliest Chinese instance where the two phrases of "sat in the open ground" and "white ox" coupled together as the expression "white ox exposed out in the open" can be traced back to the famous lay buddhist Li Tongxuan's 李通玄 (645–740) *Xin Huayan jing lun* 新華嚴經論 (Exposition on the Eighty-Fascicle Version of the Flower Ornament Scripture); see T. no. 1739, 36: 722c17–18. Later, in the Chan literature, this expression became a stable idea for the buddha way or intrinsic awakening.

20. Great *kalpa*, or *mahakalpa*, refers to the expanse of time from the birth of a universe until it is destroyed and another begins in its place. The essence of this passage means before birth and death.

21. This idea of the "truth of all dharmas as being unconcealed" (*fafa buxincang, gujin chang xianlu* 法法不隱藏, 古今常顯露) can be traced back to the *Mahaaparinirvana-sutra*; see *Daban niepan jing* 大般涅槃經 T. no. 375, 12: 630b24–c03. This passage states that the Buddha never conceals the truth of his teaching on the *tathagatagarbha*, or buddha-nature. As a set phrase, however, it is unclear how far back it goes. Certainly by the Southern Song period, many Chan masters cited it simply as "the former worthies once said" (*guren dao* 古人道); for example, see case 27 of Yuanwu Keqin's 100 *gong'an* collection, *Foguo Yuanwu chanshi Biyan lu* 佛果

圜悟禪師碧巖錄 (The Blue Cliff Record of Chan Master Foguo Yuanwu), T. no. 2003, 48: 168a15–16. For an alternative English rendering of this passage, see Thomas Cleary, *The Blue Cliff Record* (Numata Center for Buddhist Translation and Research, 1998), 154.

22. This line suggests your ability to manifest transformation bodies or *nirmanakayas*, and like a fully awakened buddha, to deliver sentient beings.

23. The literal word for this is *caotou* 草頭, which in ancient times was a placeholder for the ten thousand digits. Here "the hundreds and thousands" simply means innumerable.

24. The word rendered here as "opportunity" is *ji* 機, which has many nuances. It could mean "occasion," "hub," "axis," "mechanism," or "responsiveness of adapting to changes." Here, it refers to the function of illumination, or wisdom.

25. "Manipulating conditions" here is a rendering for *yinyuan* 夤緣, which also means "brownnosing" or "currying favor to get ahead socially."

26. Literally, it should be "illumination is without effortful illumination."

27. The literal translation of this last line, "in any direction," is "horizontal and vertical," which is a Chinese expression for one capable of moving in any direction.

28. "Truth" here literally is the way or *dao* 道. In context, it serves as a placeholder for buddha-nature. Hence, I simply rendered the word as truth.

29. Here *milun* 彌綸 is rendered as "imperial edict" because of *lun* 綸, as in *dilun* 帝綸. *Mi* 彌 means "completed." In the context of this sentence, the point is that all sentient beings are already "intrinsically awakened." This awakened nature is not something that the ancestral masters transmit, but merely point out.

30. The term here is *xinggu* 形穀, which can be understood literally as "the form of gains." Yet, the term *gu* 穀 has many meanings, one of which—*bugu* 不穀—actually means "barren," "sterile." So it could mean an appearance of being sterile. In contrast to "eternally alive" (*changhuo* 常活), I decided to render this term as "barren." This also makes sense because it is placed in contrast to "ancestor," who is the progenitor of all subsequent generations.

31. "Flowers and leaves" in Chinese is an allegory for endless, multifarious forms.

32. The "backward step" does not refer to a "meditation technique" but means one has to be careful not to move ahead, thinking one's practice is finished, or reify whatever "attainment" one has achieved. All realizations must be dropped. One has to continue the practice.

33. The center here is *huanzhong* 環中, which refers to Zhuangzi's (fourth century BCE) idea of a state of emptiness, beyond right and wrong.

34. This means that only when awakening is forgotten and complete can it be considered thorough awakening.

35. Emerging and sinking refers to birth and death.

36. This phrase "go wash your bowl" is from the seventh *gong'an* in the *Wumenguan* or the "Gateless Barrier." The story goes: One day a newly arrived monk sought out instructions from Chan master Zhaozhou, who said to the monk, "Have you had your gruel yet?" The monk replied, "I have eaten it already." Zhaozhou

retorted, "Then go wash your bowl!" The monk gained an awakening. See my book, *Passing through the Gateless Barrier* (Boulder, CO: Shambhala, 2016), 73–81; T. 48: 293c25–28.

37. Drink your tea is also an answer given by Zhaozhou, which comes from *Wudeng huiyuan* 五燈會元 (Five Flames Merging at Its Source). The story goes: Zhaozhou asked a newly arrived monk, "Have you been here before?" The monk replied, "Have arrived." Zhaozhou retorted, "Then go have some tea." Zhaozhou asked another monk and the monk replied, "Never been here." Zhaozhou also retorted, "Go have some tea." [Witnessing these episodes,] the First Seat of the monastery asked Zhaozhou, "Why did you tell the monk who has been here to have some tea and tell the monk who has never been here to also go have some tea?" Zhaozhou called out to the First Seat and the First Seat responded, "Yes!" "Go have some tea also!" said Zhaozhou.

38. "Already complete" is my rendering for *xiancheng* 現成, which is a well-known idea in Chan that everything, as it is, is already self-evident. In other words, all things inherently embody the truth of suchness and buddha-nature. In Japanese, it is pronounced *genjo* as in *genjo koan* or a case that is already self-evident.

39. Here, "this matter" (*yiduan shii* 一段事) refers to our intrinsic awakened nature.

40. The general idea of "rolling and unrolling" is the mastery of birth and death—being able to live and die at one's command.

41. "Light and luminosity" here is a rendering for *guangming* 光明, which usually refers to the function of selfless wisdom.

42. "Family style" or *jiafeng* 家風 refers to the particular style, behavior, viewpoint, and pedagogy of a Chan/Zen master or lineage. Here, it has the meaning of "the tradition of the buddhas and ancestral masters."

43. "Already self-evident and complete" is a rendering of *xiancheng*; see note 38.

44. This quote from Deshan Xuanjian 德山宣鑑 (782–865) can be found in *Jingde chuangdeng lu* 景德傳燈錄 (Transmission of the Lamp in The Jingde Era), T. no. 2076, 51: 318a02–3.

45. This expression of "sitting through the three periods of time" (*zuoduan sanji* 坐斷 三際) refers to transcending the past, present, and future through the act of sitting.

Index

ABOUT THE AUTHOR

GUO GU is a Chan teacher, author, and Buddhist scholar. He is the founder of the Tallahassee Chan Center (https://tallahasseechan.org) in Florida and of the socially engaged interdenominational Buddhist organization Dharma Relief (DharmaRelief.org). As one of the few teachers carrying on the living wisdom of Chan Buddhism in the West and as the trainer of all Western Dharma teachers in the Dharma Drum Lineage of Master Sheng Yen, Guo Gu has a unique ability to bring profound Buddhist doctrines to life through concrete methods of practice. His teachings have touched the hearts of many students across the globe through multi-day, intensive Chan retreats in different countries.

Guo Gu first learned meditation as a child in 1972 with Master Guangqin (1892–1986), one of the most respected Chinese meditation masters and ascetics in Taiwan. In 1980, Guo Gu moved to the United States and began studying with Master Sheng Yen (1931–2009). In 1991, he was ordained as a monk and became Master Sheng Yen's first personal attendant and assistant. In 1995, he experienced his first breakthrough and was given permission to teach Chan independently, representing Master Sheng Yen at his home monastery and in different parts of the world. His subsequent experiences of Chan were also recognized by other teachers in both the Chan and Japanese Zen traditions. Wanting to bring Buddhism beyond monastic walls, Guo Gu left monkhood and re-entered the world in 2000. In 2008 he received his PhD in Buddhist Studies from Princeton University and began teaching as a professor of Buddhist studies at Florida State University in Tallahassee, Florida.

Guo Gu has published several books on Chan Buddhism to make Chan teachings accessible to the West. His first book, *The Essence of Chan,* is an introduction to the theory and practice of Chan as taught by Bodhidharma (the first ancestor-master of Chan in China). A follow-up book, *Passing Through the Gateless Barrier: Koan Practice for Real Life,* is an exposition and translation of the forty-eight koans of the timeless *Gateless Barrier* (a revered collection of stories of awakening). His most recent book, *Silent Illumination: A Chan Buddhist Path to Natural Awakening,* offers instructions and translations of the writings of Hongzhi, the founder of one of the most important methods of Chan practice. Guo Gu has also edited and translated a number of Master Sheng Yen's books from Chinese to English.

Guo Gu teaches that Chan wisdom is compassion in action. Responding to the early weeks of the coronavirus pandemic, his nonprofit organization Dharma Relief formed partnerships across separate Buddhist organizations and volunteers to fundraise, purchase, and distribute over one million surgical face masks to frontline healthcare workers in North America. To learn more about the Dharma Relief initiatives that are currently underway, please visit DharmaRelief.org.